The Use of Deed Restrictions in Subdivision Development

Helen C. Monchow

SOTHIS PRESS

ISBN 978-1-0365-0656-8

This edition is published by Sothis Press © 2023. The company is registered in England and Wales. The Company Number is 14900389.

SOTHIS PRESS

Sothis Press aims to completely reimagine the public domain book with an emphasis on universal access to captivatingly designed print editions. We believe that technology will enable every single book ever published to be perpetually accessible in beautiful print form. Sothis is beauty in ubiquity.

www.sothis.press
1 Waterhouse Square, London, ECIN 2ST

The Use of Deed Restrictions in Subdivision Development

By Helen C. Monchow

Published By

The Institute for Research in Land Economics and Public Utilities

337 East Chicago Avenue

CHICAGO, ILLINOIS

1928

TABLE OF CONTENTS

FOREWORD

With this study the Institute begins the publication of two series of research monographs, one in the field of Land Economics and the other in Public Utility Economics. Heretofore, the results of research by members of the Institute staff have appeared in its own *Journal of Land and Public Utility Economics*, other periodicals and books. These series of research monographs form an intermediate way of publishing the results of its investigations. The *Journal* appears quarterly and carries short articles. The books that have been published survey a considerably larger field. The research monographs will be media for certain phases of larger research projects more ample than those covered by *Journal* articles and yet more restricted than those in books. They will be published from time to time as the material ripens rather than regularly or periodically.

Cooperative research is an established policy of the Institute. Although each individual is responsible for the research work that he does, he has full opportunity to confer with other members of the staff and obtain their suggestions and various points of view. The result is that each publication of the Institute of whatever length represents to a certain degree the combined efforts of the staff together with, in certain cases, the advice of informed persons not affiliated with the staff. This monograph is no exception to this policy.

RICHARD T. ELY, *Director,*
Institute for Research in
Land Economics and Public Utilities.

AUTHOR'S PREFACE

From the standpoint of controlling development the pattern of our modern cities is determined largely by the activities of two groups, the realtors and the city planners. Each seeks to establish through legal means the plan it has conceived for the area in question. Thus city planning, zoning and subdivision control ordinances together with private contracts in the form of deed restrictions make up the composite of control under which our cities are growing up. This study of deed restrictions represents therefore only one phase of the larger subject of control over the development of urban land.

The approach is essentially economic rather than legal, although it has been necessary to consider some of the legal problems and their economic significance. The purpose has been to consider specific control provisions and to analyze their effect (1) upon the land actually covered by the deed and (2) upon the relations between the conveyor and purchaser of the land, who are the parties to the contract. The broader implications of control through restrictions in deeds, i. e., their effect on the city pattern as a whole, have not been considered. The writer has tried to keep in mind the seller and buyer of subdivision property and to analyze and evaluate these control devices in the light of the relations between the parties to that transaction.

A further limitation, of course, lies in the relatively small number of deeds analyzed. However, the sample is fairly well scattered from the point of view of both geography and time and represents a wide range of control. In securing these deeds the writer is indebted to the National Association of Real Estate Boards for the use of material in its files, to Olmsted Brothers, landscape architects, for supplying a copy of the charted summary of restrictions on properties developed by them, and to the individual subdividers who sent sample deeds and other materials pertaining to their subdivision activities. The writer wishes specially to thank Mr. Harry E. Smoot and Mr. Charles S. Ascher, who read the manuscript, particularly those parts dealing with the legal phases, but who are in no way responsible for the opinions expressed. Finally, appreciation is due various members of the Institute staff who have offered valuable suggestions and counsel.

HELEN C. MONCHOW

Chicago, Illinois
November, 1928

CHAPTER I

Deed Restrictions in Controlling Land Development

CHICAGO'S open lake front in the heart of the city is frequently admired. Yet this stretch of land from Michigan Avenue eastward to the lake is opposite what is nearly the most valuable and intensively developed land in Chicago. The question naturally arises: How has this valuable lake front been preserved from commercial use?

The answer lies mainly in the existence of restrictions drawn for the benefit of the abutting property when it was subdivided in 1836 and 1839. At that time the land between Michigan Avenue and the lake was marked on the plats "open ground, no building" and "public ground forever to remain vacant of buildings." Since then these restrictions have been attacked repeatedly but unsuccessfully in the courts. In three decisions[1] the courts have upheld the restrictions. Briefly stated, the judicial reasoning was (1) that the owners of abutting property are entitled to an injunction against the use of the park for purposes other than those designated in the original dedication; (2) that the restrictions apply not only to the precise area referred to in the plat of the original subdivision but also to the land which has been added toward the lake; and (3) that legislation cannot divest a legal right set forth in the dedication.

Chicago's lake front is an outstanding illustration of the effectiveness of this type of control over land development, the firm legal status it has attained, and the very great influence it may exert on the city pattern. In short, the example shows the broader implications of restrictions on subdivision property.

To treat the wide variety of restrictions which are now being imposed on subdivision developments in their larger aspects, i. e., their effect on the community as a whole, would lead far afield. The scope of this study has therefore been limited to restrictions placed on residential subdivision property and a still further limitation will confine the discussion to the effect of these restrictions on the subdivider and the original purchasers of his lots.

When a lot is sold in a restricted subdivision, something more than a mere transfer of title takes place. This transaction, which lays down certain rules with regard to the use of that land, defines the relations between the subdivider and the purchaser, and frequently between the various purchasers as well. For example, a vendor may stipulate in a restrictive clause placed in the deeds of all lots in the subdivision that residences must be set back 30 feet from the lot line. The subdivider is exercising the right to dispose of his property as he sees fit, but he is bound not to overstep certain limits set by law. The lot purchasers sacrifice their right to the free use of their separate lots, but they gain the right of protecting the benefit they derive from the restriction against its violation by any of their neighbors. The rights and duties which are set forth in these restrictive clauses are all-important. The restrictions define not only what an individual may or or may not do with his property, but also how far he may go in preventing others

[1] *City of Chicago v. Ward*, 169 Ill. 392 (1897); *Bliss v. Ward*, 198 Ill. 104 (1902); *Ward v. Field Museum*, 241 Ill. 496 (1909).

from doing that which might damage his interests.

To the economist the regulation of human activities with respect to land is the important aspect of deed restrictions. Land is the basis of those relations, and transactions involving land furnish the materials for this study.

But before analyzing deed restrictions in detail, it may be well to consider their setting in relation to the general problem of controlling urban land utilization and the relation of these instruments to other types of control with which they come in contact. The purpose of this chapter, therefore, is to trace very briefly the evolution of urban land regulation, point out the need for and the major purposes of such control, as well as to explain the reasons for selecting the subdivision field as the place for studying restrictive agreements in operation. In other words, this chapter will indicate the place of deed restrictions in the developing technique of regulating urban land utilization.

The field of public control of land uses is a comparatively new activity in this country. About a quarter century ago the country suddenly awoke to the serious problems which had arisen from lack of planning. Cities were first to show symptoms of the need, and as a result the development of systematic control began about the turn of the century in this country.

Certain isolated instances of control existed prior to this time. Building codes are one form of public regulation which is of fairly long standing. But control with respect to the planning or use of the land itself lagged far behind the need for it. There were exceptions, however, such as the planning of the Federal City under the L'Enfant Plan and the planning of certain eastern towns such as Philadelphia and Williamsburg, Virginia. But such developments were ahead of time. They cannot be said actually to have been a part of the general movement toward control in accordance with a well-developed or unified plan.

Likewise in the field of private control, although from early times frequent use was made of restrictions in deeds, the device does not appear in its modern form until comparatively recent times. Properties were frequently bound by restrictions, but these were employed almost wholly as prohibitory and not as regulatory measures. Here also, of course, exceptions may be cited. As far back as 1749 William Penn's son drew up a set of restrictions which is strikingly modern in some respects. He stipulated that buildings must be of brick or stone; that houses must conform to the regulation lines of the street; that building must take place within a year after purchase if the lots were on the public square and within two years on lots on the main street beyond the square; that no patents or deeds should be issued to purchasers until buildings were up; and that the buyers must pay a ground rent of seven shillings per lot. These restrictions drawn nearly 180 years ago show an attempt at what we would term today a "community development."

But not until about 55 years ago did a development appear which may be said to be the forerunner of the modern highly restricted subdivision. At Riverside, Illinois,[2] was developed a community which used the device of control by deed restrictions in its modern sense. Land there was sold "only to an absolute settler who will agree to build immediately or within one year from the time of purchase, a home costing at

[2] Riverside Improvement Company, Riverside, 1871, *Description of Improvements, Views and Buildings.* (Chicago, 1871).

least $3,000, to be located thirty feet back from the front of the lot line, which thirty feet must be retained as an open court or dooryard."

As already stated, these are only isolated instances of control over land utilization and cannot be regarded as part of the definite movement which began about 25 or 30 years ago. Not until cities began to grow by leaps and bounds did conscious control as a more or less unified movement begin to sweep the country.

Certain fundamental characteristics of the modern city and modern city growth have made the development of a technique of regulation essential. In the first place, there is the tremendous rapidity of city growth. The facts of urbanization are familiar. The figures portraying urban growth are easily transposed into terms of more intensive as well as more extensive use of the urban area. The eye pictures more and taller apartments and a constantly increasing acreage in the process of transition from agricultural to urban use. Both of these pictures point out the greatly enlarged opportunities for the exercise of control over urban expansion, particularly over the outlying areas which are most plastic.

Secondly, modern engineering progress has made decentralization of our cities possible. From the point of view of control two problems are created as a result of technological improvement. Improved transportation has made it possible for more people to have access to a given area, such as the loop in Chicago. Herein lies a problem in congestion which requires the exercise of public authority. On the other hand, improved transportation has greatly expanded the urban area. Suburban growth brings with it the problem of regulating development adjacent to a city in the interests of the future expansion of that city, as well as problems of administration arising out of the possibility of conflict among neighboring political jurisdictions.

The third need for control is to be found in the rapid rate of production of urban land. It has long been suspected that areas were being subdivided and sold far in excess of demand as measured by population growth. But only very recently have steps been taken to measure quantitatively the relation between population and areas ready for urban use.[3] As soon as adequate facts of this nature are available, they will serve as a basis for a more scientific control. It should not be overlooked in this connection, however, that production of urban land must of necessity take place to a certain extent in anticipation of demand. By production of land is meant the bringing of land into use for a specific purpose. Production is used here in the economic sense to mean the creation of utilities. According to this usage, production of land consists of releasing the services of a given area for a particular use, or changing that area from one use to another. For example, production of urban land consists of transforming acreage (often in agricultural use) into building lots, and urban land, like most other commodities, is subject to the economies of large-scale production. It would be uneconomical to add lots to the urban area singly or in groups of two or three, whenever an individual or two wanted to buy a building site. Economic development of urban land requires that a considerable tract be purchased, subdivided and improved as a unit. This does not alter the

[3] See Orman S. Fink and Coleman Woodbury, "Area Requirements of Cities in the Region of Chicago," 4 *Journal of Land & Public Utility Economics* 273–282 (August, 1928).

fact, however, that a certain balance should be maintained between population and expansion of the urban area, and some means of public control is necessary to assure a proper relationship between the two.

Finally, private initiative alone is not adequate to control expansion of the urban area. Regulations of one kind or another are being applied to an increasing number of our activities, in an attempt to safeguard the interests of the many and thus protect the institution of liberty.

The conflict of interests between individuals or individuals and groups is the reason for the increased control over private initiative, and this restraint is particularly necessary in transactions involving land. Land has certain peculiar characteristics which make regulation of its development all the more important. Relatively land has a greater fixity of investment than do other forms of capital goods, a feature arising chiefly from the improvements erected on the land. Not only are the improvements themselves relatively permanent, but they very definitely and for a considerable time determine the character of the utilization of land. Fixed improvements, whose services extend over a long period of years, make it doubly necessary to see that individuals act in harmony with a larger plan than that dictated by their own immediate interests. Furthermore, these acts concern not only those who commit them, but their neighbors as well, for separate units of land are extremely interdependent, and susceptible to outside influences. The erection of an inharmonious structure on one lot affects not only the value of that particular site but the adjacent ones as well, and frequently the entire block. Therefore, control of one sort or another is necessary to insure a desirable city pattern, and this control to be effective should be exercised over a relatively large area and in accordance with a long-time point of view.

These evidences of the need for control may be summed up in a single statement. The process of urbanization has so increased the number and complexity of the relationships arising out of the use and title to urban land that measures of control have become absolutely essential to the economic functioning of urban life.

The major part of this control is exercised with respect to the physical development of the urban area. This is true not only of deed restrictions but of other forms of regulation as well. The greater proportion of restrictive agreements have to do with the type and use of the structures and the use of the lot area. The relationships between the seller and the buyers of subdivision land are expressed mainly in terms of what the latter may not do in the matter of building construction, lot layout, etc. In other words, control as it is exercised by a public or private agency consists largely of regulations in the nature of land planning. This fact gives a basis for outlining the purposes of control in planning terms.

The regulation of urban land utilization has three general purposes. It aims first at the prevention of waste. In this connection control consists mainly in planning which may prevent a great many forms of useless expenditure. It may prevent waste of buildings, by prohibiting the erection of structures in mapped streets.[4] These buildings would

[4] Prevention of building in mapped streets is one of the major problems in preserving the city plan. Considerable difference of opinion exists as to whether the more effective instrument of control in this case is the police power or eminent domain. The former is ad-

(Continued on page 5

eventually have to be destroyed or else would necessitate the modification of the plan to a less economical arrangement. Planning may prevent waste by forestalling the division of land into units which cannot be profitably utilized. Finally, planning may be a time-saver by so arranging street layouts that they will facilitate movement from one part of the city to another. Careful planning with such aims as these constitutes one aspect of control.

Secondly, control seeks to stabilize land values, and, it may be, to enhance land values. These results are obtained through a form of restraint which establishes the character of a given area. If an area is set aside for residential purposes, its values are protected against a decline which might come through the intrusion of a manufacturing or commercial use into that district. Control which promotes values frequently accomplishes this end through the securing of amenities.

The third aim of control is to promote the amenities in land utilization, as well as health and general welfare. This purpose is becoming increasingly important. Instead of being looked upon as idealistic and impractical, or as a sort of sentimental goal of the uplifters, it is coming to be recognized as having substantial economic value. People are willing to pay for amenities and therefore they have a market value which, apart from the desirability of improving housing standards, justifies the measures taken to secure them.

In the light of these purposes it is obvious that control can best be exercised and can be most effective if applied when land is produced. Planning is always superior to replanning and this is particularly true in considering the peculiar characteristics of land. It is not necessary to dwell upon the obvious fact that land once utilized for a given purpose assumes a fairly definite character which is difficult and expensive to change. The economic characteristics of land, including fixity of investment, scarcity of land of a particular class, the situs element and the long-time effect of any improvements on the land, show how essential it is that the proper utilization should be determined as accurately as possible when land of a certain kind is produced.

The chief commercial producers of urban land in general are the subdividers. They take acreage, subdivide it and put it on the market for urban use. They lay out street systems and frequently they specify and establish through the device of deed restrictions the use to which the lots shall be put. They definitely determine the general character of the area and in so doing they greatly influence the pattern of the municipality. From one point of view the municipality may be looked upon as an aggregate of subdivisions, and therefore the activities of subdividers and the methods they employ are of the first importance in a consideration of the control over land utilization.

The conditions under which the subdivider exercises his control vary according to the location of his subdivision. The relationships he establishes with the purchasers of his lots are influenced by the presence or absence of established relationships between him and the public authorities. The production of residential subdivision land frequently takes place outside the corporate limits of a municipality or outside its jurisdic-

---

Footnote 4 continued from page 4)
vocated and practiced in New York (New York Laws of 1926, Ch. 690, Sec. 35). The latter, known as the Massachusetts method, is proposed in the Standard City Planning Enabling Act (Secs. 21–25, incl.) and has been adopted in the California Planning Act of 1927 (California Statutes of 1927, Ch. 874, Secs. 23–25, incl.).

tion, and unless the tract is within the jurisdiction of a region organized for planning purposes, there is no public control over subdivision. If, therefore, the subdivider wishes to assure a certain character to his development, he must institute his own system of regulation, and deed restrictions are his most useful instruments. However, his freedom from planning control by public authority does not mean that he can be totally oblivious to it. This planning control often regulates the utilization of land, if not directly adjoining his tract, at least of land through which he has access to his subdivision. He is thus subject to the indirect, if not to the direct, influences of public control.

If the subdivision is located within the limits of a municipality or other political unit, the subdivider is subject to its jurisdiction and the rules and regulations which it may impose. For example, if he is operating in an area which is zoned by public authority, the restrictions which he imposes must be in harmony with the zoning system. But whether the subdivider begins his operations unhampered or unassisted by public regulation, or whether he sets his own standards, the significant point is that the subdivision is the starting point for both public and private control and it affords excellent opportunity for considering the relation between the two.

As already hinted, public and private control are not mutually exclusive. A single piece of property may be subject at the same time to both public and private restrictions. While a subdivider frequently controls his development through restrictive covenants in conveyances, that area may also be subject to regulations by some public agency. Subsequently deed restrictions will be compared more fully with zoning ordinances as regulatory devices, and it is pertinent here to point out only the basic difference between public and private control.

This difference lies in the relative *intensivity* of their control. Public restrictions cannot be used to discriminate arbitrarily between individuals. They must be applicable to all persons within the jurisdiction of the political unit which imposes them or all persons within the group regulated. Therefore, they must not set requirements that are beyond the power of the economically weakest members of the group to satisfy. For example, a subdivision control ordinance in establishing the width of building lots must consider the smallest income groups and set a lot-width which will not result in a price prohibitory to that group. In short, public control can set only marginal standards. A statement to this effect by a protagonist of public control is particularly interesting:

> "In directing the type of subdivision a distinct limitation exists upon the power of official planning, as residing in legislative bodies and exercised upon the advice of planning commissions. In subdivision control official planning usually can demand no more than the obvious type of subdivision, since this usually represents the average. The work of a planning commission can constantly tend toward establishing the standards of a high type of subdivision, but the mediocre subdivider will ever rest upon the average in his conception of choice in the exercise of property rights."[5]

Subdividers who wish to establish developments with additional requirements must resort to private control to insure this development.

A subdivision enterprise, like any other organization, operates in accordance with working rules. The transactions of those participating in the en-

[5] Hugh R. Pomeroy, "Subdivision in Relation to Community Building," 3 *Annals of Real Estate Practice*, (Chicago: National Association of Real Estate Boards, 1925) p. 268.

terprise are guided not only by rules which have been developed from within the organization but also by certain rules imposed from without.

These working rules, which govern the activities of the subdivider but are not of his own making, may also conveniently be divided into private and public regulations. Chief among the instruments of private control are the restrictions contained in the deeds to the property prior to the acquisition of title by the subdivider. In other words, the land to be subdivided may be covered by restrictions inserted in previous conveyances. Such limitations are most likely to be found on land in or very near the city. They would seldom be a factor in the development of the more remote suburban subdivisions. Whenever such limitations do exist, they constitute a part of the working rules governing the activity of the subdivider.

The working rules imposed by public agencies are more frequently encountered by the subdivider. The four major types of regulation, which may serve as working rules for the subdivider, are building codes, zoning ordinances, subdivision control ordinances and regulations pertaining to "metes and bounds" subdividing. For purposes of this discussion the chief significance of the first three of these forms of control is in the minimum standards which they set for the subdivider. Building codes set minimums for the construction of improvements; zoning ordinances set minimums by prescribing the lowest uses permissible in certain districts; and subdivision control ordinances set minimums for lot requirements and utility installation. Regulations with reference to "metes and bounds" subdividing usually require the subdivider to sell his lots from a recorded map rather than by description. These forms of public regulation mark the starting point for control over land development.

In addition to these working rules imposed on the subdivider by public authority, he may set up other requirements which will be binding on both himself and the purchasers of his lots. Regulations of this kind are usually put in the form of restrictive clauses inserted in the deeds conveying the property. They set forth the rights and duties of both the subdivider and the purchasers with respect to the land conveyed. They regulate the relationships between the parties to the transfer, and these are the relationships with which this study is primarily concerned. The increasing use of deed restrictions as a means of controlling land utilization—particularly residential subdivision land—warrants some study of the forms this type of control may take, the objects it has in view and the effectiveness of the device as a measure of control.

CHAPTER II

The Developer's Plan as a Basis for Deed Restrictions

"IT is the Realtor subdivider who is really planning our cities today, who is the actual city planner in practice."[1] This statement is particularly interesting because it comes from Mr. George B. Ford, a city planner of wide reputation and a former president of the National Conference on City Planning. Subdividers take the raw land, carve out a street system, parcel the area into lots and through their development activities stamp them with a definite character. In the past, this has taken place with a minimum of interference or guidance from the neighboring city and often without any guidance at all. Now, although cities and regions are awakening to the desirability of controlling their outlying undeveloped areas, it may still be said that the subdividers are in large measure determining the pattern of our cities and they are likely to continue to do so for some time to come. Hence, the developer's plan for his subdivision is of far-reaching significance in the development of the urban area and in the use of deed restrictions.

The developer's plan, as the term is used here, is the scheme for the physical layout of the area, including the improvements necessary to make the lots ready for building purposes and indications of the placement and general nature of the structures to be erected thereon. In other words, developer's planning consists of working out and providing for the necessary details of construction and regulation which will make possible the fulfillment of his conception of that subdivision as a balanced development. Or, as one writer has put it, "Planning should be so thorough as to offer an accurate outline and picture of the project to be completed."

From this description of the developer's plan it is plain that this discussion is not concerned with bare subdivision which consists of the mere platting and staking out of lots. A distinction is drawn between a "subdivision" and a "subdivision development." The latter includes, beside the parcelling of the area into building sites, the preparation of those lots for use. "Sale for use" and not for speculative purposes is the aim of subdivision development. Subdivision development illustrates the broadening scope of the subdivider's activity. In a carefully planned subdivision the developer must exercise the functions himself or secure the services of a city planner, a landscape architect, an engineer and a building architect.

For purposes of describing the details of developer's planning it will be most convenient to suppose that the plan is being imposed upon an area which is not within the jurisdiction of a municipality or region which is exercising planning control. This assumption will facilitate the discussion for it permits the inclusion of all the main functions which a subdivider may be called on to perform. It also obviates the necessity for repeated qualifications in the form of public regulation of subdivision activities.

Therefore, the following description of the developer's plan will be based on

[1] "City Planning and Unbuilt Outlying Areas," 3 *Annals of Real Estate Practice* (Chicago: National Association of Real Estate Boards, 1925), p. 247.

the assumption that the subdivider is responsible for the development of the area. It is not a description of an actual plan or a proposal for a model plan. It is merely an outline of the most important items to be considered in planning a subdivision development.

The subdivider's control consists of his plan for the area and the restrictions which he places in his conveyances to insure the fulfillment of that plan. The plan is the initial step.

The first step toward careful planning is a thorough and painstaking survey of the area to be developed, including contours, relief maps, air maps, etc. From these sources the developer can gather detailed information about his subdivision — the irregularities in its topography, the location of trees, monuments, etc. The facts gleaned from such surveys are necessary as a basis on which to rest his plan of development. They provide the data, for example, for determining the drainage system, the grading of streets, the proper location of utility lines and sewers. A street plan which is superimposed on a hilly area without reference to contours is a costly improvement. The same is true of a plan which in the process of platting and staking destroys the natural growth on the land and then calls for the expenditure of considerable sums for trees and shrubbery to beautify parkways. With full information on such points the developer is enabled to plan his subdivision more economically and more attractively. He can lay out his streets and utility lines in harmony with the contour of the land, thus saving expense and at the same time increasing the attractiveness of his development. He can plan his lot layout in such a way as to take maximum advantage of the distinctive physical features of his tract. In short, let the contour dictate the plan as far as possible, instead of trying to run the plan counter to it and thus creating streets and lots that are not usable because the grades are too steep and the expense of improvement is too great. Complete surveys are therefore a valuable prerequisite to the developer's plan.

The survey idea should be applied not only to the physical area of the subdivision itself. The effect of contour of the land, as well as size of the tract, on the developer's plan is obvious. Not so obvious but quite as important from the point of view of layout is the relation of the subdivision to the surrounding area, which should also be determined by careful survey. Four factors in this relationship may be mentioned: (1) distance from the neighboring city; (2) transport facilities; (3) character of the neighboring city; and (4) character of the proposed development. The following paragraphs will point out some of the ways in which these factors influence the developer's plan for his subdivision.

The effect of the distance of the development from the city of influence is clear. Developments at a distance from the city take on a distinctly suburban character and a new kind of development called "estate type" is growing in popularity with certain income groups. On the other hand, subdivisions nearer the city are for obvious reasons cut up into smaller lots and developed for different uses. But distance from the city is measured not only in miles but in time and price. This latter method of measurement ties the distance factor to the transport factor. Measurement of distance in time and price has a very direct bearing on the development of outlying areas.

One result of the improvement of transport facilities has been to bring the outlying regions within the reach of the smaller income groups whose demand for home sites must be satisfied by smaller lots. Lot sizes are not the only item in the developer's plan to be affected by this changing demand. The distribution of uses and the community features will be markedly different as a result.

The effect of the character of the neighboring city is perhaps not so obvious but quite as important. A plan for a tract located just outside the town of Harvey, Illinois, would naturally be quite different from the plan for a development outside of Evanston, Illinois. Suppose both developments were being planned for what is coming to be known as the "junior executive" group. But even though the same purchasing group was appealed to, the plan for the developments would differ markedly. The subdivision outside of Evanston could rely upon the extensive use of Evanston's well-developed shopping center, whereas in the other area provision would have to be made for more adequate shopping facilities of the kind to appeal to the tastes of the prospective purchasers.

The influence of the character of the proposed development upon the subdivider's planning is also plain. To illustrate: community features are vastly more important in a subdivision for a low income group; the plans for the improvements will of course differ greatly with the presence or absence of apartment or business uses; developments for the higher income groups afford opportunities for a greater variety of lot patterns and block layouts. These examples merely suggest the close relationship existing between the character of the proposed development and the developer's plan for the physical layout of the area.

These four factors, along with the contour and size of the tract, are fixed by the selection of the area to be subdivided. Together they determine the developer's plan. The various items in that plan will vary in number and importance according to these general characteristics of the subdivision and its surroundings. Description of these factors also emphasizes the fact that no rules-of-thumb can be applied to subdivision planning. Each subdivision is a problem in itself, to be worked out under the influence of the conditions in the region within which it lies.

The variable items in the developer's plan may now be considered separately. The first concern of the developer is to give careful consideration to the area surrounding his subdivision. His plan will be affected in three major respects by his surroundings: (1) His subdivision forms part of a regional development. He is therefore concerned with the status of the surrounding land, its present development or lack of it and its probable future. A knowledge of the region will enable him to fit his plan into the whole scheme or, if need be, protect his plan as far as possible against deteriorating influences. (2) Of particular importance are the uses of the land immediately adjoining his tract. Even the existence of a zoning system is not absolute assurance that the subdivision will not be endangered from without. An adjoining development may be meeting the requirements of the zoning provisions and still have standards so low as to endanger a proposed high-class development adjacent to it. Then there is the possibility that the tract in question might be on the verge of a different utilization. This raises the border problem which is one of the difficulties of zoning. So whether he is near a zoned area or not, the subdivider will do well to look to the protection of the borders of his development. A solution that has been tried both by subdividers and by municipalities is the planning of parkways as buffers between different use zones or between adjoining developments. One subdivider has so placed his golf course as to surround his development almost completely. (3) The third problem in the relationship of the subdivision to the surrounding area is that of street connections and traffic movement. This is important not merely from the point of view of access to the subdivision itself but also from the point of view of the movement of traffic in the entire area. In the first place, the streets of the new subdivision are required to connect with existing streets without jogs. This is the point on which public control, wherever it is exercised, is most insistent. Then where the natural path of major thoroughfares or arterial highways lies through the proposed new development, adequate provision should be made for their extension. In this way the subdivision is coordinated with the radial growth of the city and the plan for traffic movement in the region of which it is a part.

Street plans within the subdivision fall into two groups: major streets and minor streets. The former are the heavy traffic streets which connect the subdivision with the surrounding area. These streets should be relatively straight, providing the most direct routes to the main termini. Adequate width and special construction to bear this kind of traffic are the other points of importance. The minor streets are the flexible elements in the street plan. They are mainly within the subdivision and are designed primarily for the service of the lot owners. Width and type of construction are important considerations, largely from the point of view of economy. Minor streets may be relatively narrow because one of the aims is to discourage traffic through them in the interest of more peace and quiet for the lot owners and greater safety for children. Naturally their construction need not be so heavy nor so expensive as that of the major streets. The increasing use of curves and the occasional introduction of cul-de-sacs are adding greatly to the attractiveness of the better-planned subdivision. Under this heading also belongs provision for alleys, lanes, footways, bridle paths, etc., as well as the sidewalks and parkways bordering the streets. The adaptation of the street plan to contours has already been touched upon and need only be mentioned here for the sake of emphasis.

After laying out the street plan the developer turns next to the apportionment of uses in his subdivision. In such apportionment he exercises a zoning power. If he is developing a purely residential subdivision, the question arises whether to permit apartments or multi-family units of any kind. If the subdivision is large, then provision for a shopping center is essential. The subdivider must decide not only which of these uses he will permit, but where they shall be located and how much land he will allocate to each type of use. The location of the business area, if any, is usually more or less predetermined. Its natural place is at the juncture of the main traffic streets in or bounding the subdivision. Its amount, however, should be determined with careful reference to the population it will serve.

Research methods are being applied to this problem and are revealing the relationship which exists in certain fully developed areas between business frontage and numbers of residents. Such measurements available to the subdivider form a basis for intelligent planning of business frontage.[2] Other considerations in connection with the platting of business frontage are the size and shape of the lots and plans for control of the type of buildings to be erected thereon. Subdividers have awakened to the knowledge that shopping centers need not be blots upon the subdivision landscape. If care is taken and control exercised, the store buildings may be constructed to harmonize with the whole development and not impair even the most exclusive subdivision.

The next step in the developer's zoning will probably be the location of the multi-family units. These too will follow the major streets and boundaries of the subdivision, serving as buffers for the single-family residential uses which it is assumed will be the main interest of the subdivider. The most frequent practice in a large subdivision is to place the large apartments near the borders of the tract, with the two- and three-family dwellings next inside and the single-family residences in the interior of the development. It might be noted here that a new departure in subdividing is the development exclusively devoted to apartment buildings. Subdivisions of this variety create new problems in lot layout, street planning, and improvement installation.

The single-family residence lots will be located in the most desirable sections of the subdivision. In planning their location the developer will seek to exploit to the utmost any distinctive physical features his tract may contain. By so doing he creates amenity values, which will repay him for his care in planning.

The subdivider may further use his zoning powers to establish architectural districts. Examples of this type of planning are found mainly on the Pacific Coast, where subdividers are pioneering in architectural control. The developers of Palos Verdes Estates in Los Angeles County have worked out a most elaborate system for regulating architecture.[3] Their method is to establish districts for architecture of specified types, which are defined in terms of the color of the structures, their material and the type of roof. Four such districts are established and zoning is also involved in that business lots are all located in "Type IV Architecture District." The potentialities of this type of control have yet to be tested. Architectural control would seem to be more important in subdivisions where the lots are comparatively small, for there the structures are closer together and the chance for clash between too inharmonious types is greater.

After determining lot uses the developer plans his lot layout which, of course, must be coordinated with the proposed utilization of the land. Lot sizes should be determined with careful attention to area as well as to width and depth. On single-family residence lots the aim is to secure as much individuality as possible without impractical layouts. Adequate platting also includes the placing of building lines and easements for the installation of the utilities and the location of structures. The platting of building lines is quite as important as provisions for adequate lot size, for the latter may go for naught if the place of the structure on the lot is not regulated with reference to the plat as a whole. The complexity of the problem of establishing building lines is reflected in the detailed character of the deed restrictions covering this point.

[2] See Coleman Woodbury, "The Size of Retail Business Districts in the Chicago Metropolitan Region," 4 *Journal of Land & Public Utility Economics*, 85–91 (February, 1928).

[3] See Protective Restrictions, Palos Verdes Estates, Los Angeles County, California. Tract 7333 and Tract 8652, Montemalaga.

The planning of the improvements constitutes one of the most important items in the developer's scheme. Improvements may be divided roughly into three groups. The first improvements include clearing the tract, draining it and installing culverts and bridges, grading the streets and curbing them, and placing street signs. The second group may be described as the underground improvements which should be installed before paving. This group includes sewer, water and gas lines and in the better subdivisions electric and telephone lines as well. In addition to providing for the location of these lines under the streets this group also requires plans for their connection with the separate lots. To take care of this point the developer's plan should include the mapping of an easement on the rear of each lot to permit the entrance of these utilities to the individual lots. The third group of improvements includes the paving of the streets, the laying of sidewalks and the planting of trees. The developer's plan for these improvements should give attention not only to their location but also to the quality of the improvements.

Finally, an adequate developer's plan will provide the necessary community features. School sites are among the most important. Location is one major consideration and ample space is the other. The remaining community features may be grouped under the head of recreational areas. By recreational areas are meant only the smaller open spaces, not large tracts such as the public parks in our large cities. These recreational areas may be public or private, as the subdivider may decide. They may be dedicated to the city which will then maintain them or they may be designated for the use of the lot purchasers who will be charged for their upkeep. This point has little bearing on the planning aspect. The main thing is to see that adequate recreational areas are provided. Considerable difference of opinion exists as to what is "adequate" but 10% of the gross area of the subdivision is probably not too high a figure. Of course, for a very small development this might be excessive but the suggestion has been made that small, adjacent subdivisions might solve the difficulty by joining in providing the necessary recreational areas. The provision of these facilities is particularly desirable in the subdivisions for the lower income groups, but cost has been supposed to make this impossible. The recent researches of Mr. Robert Whitten, however, seem to indicate that careful planning can make these advantages available for the less expensive subdivisions.[4]

In addition to the playgrounds in connection with the schools there is need for play spaces for the smaller children. These areas need not be large but should be comparatively numerous and so placed that the children will not have to go long distances or cross main traffic streets to reach them. In some subdivisions this need has been filled by a lot layout which is described as the "interior parkway." This type of layout is by block rather than by lot, for the houses face the interior of the block with their garages on the street frontage. In one such development the whole block is 353 feet deep and each lot owner has 125 feet of lot depth for his own use, the balance being developed as a park for all the owners in the block. This layout not only supplies one solution of the problem of play spaces for small children but also increases privacy.

[4] See "A Research into the Economics of Land Subdivision," School of Citizenship and Public Affairs of Syracuse University and the Regional Plan of New York and Its Environs, 1927.

Parks may serve other purposes than providing play space for children. An occasional open space adds to the beauty of the subdivision and affords an opportunity for using odd-shaped pieces of land that frequently occur in cutting up a tract.

Golf courses are increasingly common adjuncts, particularly of subdivisions remote from the city. From the control point of view, their usefulness as buffers between the subdivision and inharmonious uses has already been mentioned. They also preserve a large open space on one or more sides of the development and this is always an asset to a residential district.

The developer's plan as outlined here has been confined largely to a description of the physical layout of the area. The purposes of such planning are to secure economies in development and to secure the maximum amenities that can be derived from the area. Translated into terms of value, the subdivider seeks through planning to create and protect land values. A third purpose of planning is to visualize the completed project in order to be assured that the best use of the property is being planned before improvement actually begins. Some subdividers even go so far as to make miniature models of the tract, together with papier mache reproductions of some of the proposed improvements. Still another method of insuring suitable development is to stake out the plan roughly on the ground. This permits readjustment where change seems desirable.

According to the definition set forth at the beginning of this chapter, the "developer's plan" includes more than the outline of the physical layout of the area. An adequate plan includes a scheme for the improvements to be constructed on the area, as well as detailed platting. Careful planning will go for naught, if building takes place in a haphazard fashion and without reference to a definite scheme, for the structures to be built on the subdivision will determine in large measure the character of the development.

Therefore, the subdivider seeks to make certain that development shall be in harmony with his platting scheme and shall take place in accordance with his plans for the area. To this end he draws restrictions to be inserted in the deeds conveying the separate parcels. In this way he can insure through a legal instrument that the open spaces he has planned will be maintained, that buildings will not encroach upon his carefully planned street vistas, that inharmonious structures will not mar the appearance of the subdivision—in short, that the development will have the character which he planned for it. Thus, deed restrictions may be looked upon as a means of crystallizing the developer's plan for his subdivision.

Two general methods of imposing restrictions on building lots may be mentioned here. Restrictions may be drawn for each lot as it is sold or restrictions may be drawn for all the lots as a part of the scheme for the development of the entire area. The former method may be described roughly as aimed to promote the interests of the subdivider through more rapid turnover. Piecemeal restricting is incidental to the merchandising aspect of the subdivision function and not to the control phase. The latter method, while also in harmony with the interests of the subdivider, has the benefit of the whole area as its aim. Restrictions of this class are frequently filed with the plat of subdivision, in which case, however, the list on the plat is not a complete record of the restrictions actually inserted in the deeds conveying the property. The plat usually records only those restrictions that have to do with the physical development of the area and does not include such items as restraints on occupancy, etc. However, restrictions designated on a plat are recognized by the courts, even though they may not be referred to in the deed. In an Illinois case[5] the court held that purchasers of subdivision lots, the plat of which contained a building line, took title subject to that building line, whether their deeds referred to the building line or not. On the other hand, when restrictive clauses in deeds modify the restrictions as recorded on the plat, then the provisions in the deed prevail.[6]

For obvious reasons the piecemeal method of imposing restrictions is not desirable. In the first place, it is not conducive to harmonious development. In order to sell a certain lot the subdivider will be tempted to make a concession to satisfy some whim of his customer. For example, the privilege to violate the front building line may completely destroy the appearance of a given block. Or permission to erect an apartment house on a corner lot will ruin the effectiveness of restrictions drawn to preserve the amenities of single-family residential sites. These examples will suffice to show the unsatisfactory nature of piecemeal restrictions. As a method of *control* their usefulness is questionable.

However, one argument that may be advanced in favor of piecemeal restrictions should be considered. It may be argued that this method affords an opportunity for elasticity; or, in other words, that somewhat different restrictions may be imposed on different lots, and this may be desirable from the point of view of attractive development. But the method of drawing restrictions for the entire plat does not necessarily mean uniform restrictions. In fact, in many of the high-class developments provision is made for the different treatment of different lots, or groups of lots. By this method it is possible to have elasticity in restrictive agreements and at the same time have adequate control.

The second method of imposing restrictions coordinates them with the plan for the subdivision. The coordination process is mutually beneficial to the plan and to the restrictive agreement. A plan gains through restrictions that are drawn to assure its execution and restrictions gain prestige in the courts when they are based on a plan. This study is confined to an analysis of deed restrictions of this class, because they represent a definite attempt at the control of land development.

The usefulness and desirability of deed restrictions in insuring the developer's plan are generally granted. They constitute the means of enforcing a plan of development. But because of the binding nature of restrictive agreements and the considerable periods of time for which they are established, the courts exercise great caution in interpreting contracts of this nature and circumscribe them carefully lest they infringe too much upon the rights of the individual in his land, or impose stipulations not in harmony with the general interest.

---

[5] "Where a deed refers to a plat or subdivision, the particular descriptions shown upon such plat or subdivision are as much a part of the deed as though they were recited in it." *Simpson v. Mikkelsen*, 196 Ill. 575 at 579 (1902).

[6] *Eckhart v. Irons*, 128 Ill. 568 (1889).

CHAPTER III

The Legal Aspects of Deed Restrictions

The purpose of this chapter is to sketch broadly the legal background on which deed restrictions rest and to call attention to some fundamental principles which should be observed in the construction of restrictive clauses. It is not proposed to give an exhaustive treatment of the legal foundations and legal peculiarities of deed restrictions.

Even to outline the most significant legal features of deed restrictions is both difficult and dangerous. It is difficult because of the great complexity of the law of real property and restrictive agreements form but a small fraction of the whole. It is dangerous in that any generalization is more or less inaccurate and misleading, because the laws of the several states and the attitudes of their courts vary so widely. For example, in a number of states a restriction prohibiting the sale of certain property to, or the occupancy of certain property by, persons not of the Caucasian race is valid. But California regards the first prohibition as a restraint upon alienation which is forbidden by its Civil Code.[1] The case of *Los Angeles Investment Company* v. *Gary*[2] involved a prohibition against both alienation to and occupancy by non-Caucasians which was to be in operation until January 1st, 1930. The court ruled on both points.

> "The condition that the property be not sold, leased, or rented to one not of Caucasian birth is clearly a restraint on alienation. The deed likewise purports to convey the fee, and an incident of an estate in fee is the right of free disposal and transfer. The condition therefore is repugnant to the interest created . . . Our conclusion is that the condition against occupation of the property by anyone not of the Caucasian race is valid."

Therefore, in California any restriction which discriminates in this way must confine itself to a prohibition against "use and occupancy," not against alienation. This illustration merely emphasizes the fact that rules-of-thumb cannot be applied in a treatment of deed restrictions.

A deed has been variously defined. The broad definition[3] of a deed as a contract under seal and delivered is discarded here in favor of a definition which defines the more specific uses of the term as it is found in the law of real property: "A deed is the instrument by which the absolute title, or interest, in real estate is transferred from the grantor, or owner, to the grantee, or purchaser."[4]

---

[1] Civil Code, par. 711. "Conditions restraining alienation, when repugnant to the interest created, are void." However, in the Alien Land Law (G. L., Act. 261) initiated and approved by electors, November 2, 1920, aliens ineligible for citizenship may own or lease real estate as provided by treaty between the United States and foreign powers, and *not otherwise*. As amended in May, 1927, Act 261, Sec. 9a, the burden of proving eligibility to citizenship was placed on the alien. The 1920 statute was upheld as constitutional in *Porterfield v. Webb*, 263 U. S. 225 (1923), which involved a lease of agricultural land to a Japanese. An interesting question is whether a condition restraining alienation to a non-Caucasian who is ineligible for citizenship would be valid, unless contrary to treaty stipulations, despite the general prohibition of the Civil Code.

[2] 181 Cal. 680, 186 Pac. 596 (1919). The case involved persons of African descent.

[3] William C. Robinson, *Elementary Law* (Boston: Little, Brown and Co., 1910) sec. 129. "A *deed* is a writing sealed and delivered between the parties;" see also Bouvier's Law Dictionary (Rawle's Edition, St. Paul: West Publishing Co., 1914), "DEED. A written instrument under seal, containing a contract or agreement which has been delivered by the party to be bound and accepted by the obligee or covenantee."

[4] Nathan William MacChesney, *Principles of Real Estate Law* (New York: Macmillan Co., 1927) p. 838.

The essential parts of a deed, as usually enumerated, are the premises, the *habendum*, the *tenendum*, the *reddendum* and the conclusion. The *habendum* and *tenendum* are now obsolete.[5] Even the premises and the conclusion are relatively uniform and perfunctory; their form and general content are predetermined. The *reddendum*, therefore, which contains the covenants and conditions imposed by the grantor, is the most important part of the deed from the point of view of control over land development. This section constitutes the flexible and dynamic portion of the instrument. The clauses can be formulated—within the limits of the law, of course—to exercise whatever degree of control is desired. It might be mentioned at this point, however, that restrictions may be created by other instruments than deeds, provided a valuable consideration is involved.[6] The contract of sale is the medium most commonly used, when the deed is not the vehicle for the restrictions.

As already stated, the right to create deed restrictions rests upon the right of free contract. It is generally conceded that in conveying real estate the grantor may, within certain limits, impose restrictions on the use of that property. In the case of *Eckhart* v. *Irons*[7] the court states a position which is fairly typical when it says:

"The power of the grantor to thus impose limitations and restrictions upon the use and enjoyment of the property granted, as he may deem proper, and of the grantee to accept the same, cannot be denied, unless opposed to public policy."

Occasionally the courts have gone so far as to describe this right to enter into restrictive agreements as "unquestionable."[8]

The right to enter into restrictive agreements, however, is not unrestrained. Two major limitations may be cited. Restrictions may not be (1) contrary to public policy,[9] or (2) "unreasonable,"[10] used in its legal sense. The general principle has been established that individuals in their agreements cannot bind themselves to do that which is "injurious to the public or against the public good."[11] This definition of what is opposed to public policy, as a limitation on the power of a grantor to impose restrictions, presents only the negative aspects. One of the cases already cited states the requirement from the positive side: "Such a restriction on the use of real estate, where it does not appear that either some individual or the public would be benefited by it, would be contrary to public policy and void."[12] In other words, according to the test established here, someone must be definitely benefited by the restriction; otherwise it is invalid as against public policy.

"Reasonableness" is frequently set up as a limitation upon the drafting of restrictive agreements. The term "rea-

[5] *Ibid.*, p. 63.

[6] "The fact that the restriction is created in an instrument independent of the deed conveying title is of no consequence, as long as there is a valuable consideration moving to and from the signers." *Erichsen v. Tapert*, 172 Mich. 457 at 463 (1912).

[7] 128 Ill. 568 at 579 (1889); see also *Frye v. Partridge*, 82 Ill. 267 (1876).

[8] *Cooperative Vineyards Co. v. Ft. Stockton Irrigated Lands Co.*, 158 S. W. 1191 (Tex. Civ. App.) (1913); *Schoonmaker v. Heckscher*, 171 N. Y. App. Div. 148, 157 N. Y. Supp. 75 (1916).

[9] *Mitchell v. Leavitt*, 30 Conn. 587 (1862); *Hutchinson v. Ulrich*, 145 Ill. 336 (1893); *Cooperative Vineyards Co. v. Ft. Stockton Irrig. Lands Co.*, *supra* n. 8.

[10] *Schoonmaker v. Heckscher*, *supra* n. 8.

[11] See Bouvier's Law Dictionary, *op. cit.*, article on "Public Policy;" also article on "Void," "a contract binding the maker to do something opposed to the public policy of the state or nation, or which conflicts with the wants, interest, or prevailing sentiment of the people, or our obligations to the world, or is repugnant to the morals of the times, is void, however solemnly the same may be made."

[12] *Mitchell v. Leavitt*, *supra* n. 9.

sonableness" in law means more than moderation. Rationality is one test of the legal concept of "reasonableness," but the courts often apply an additional standard. An action may be considered reasonable if it is just according to the judgment of the average man, if it is what the average man would expect to happen under the circumstances. This test is applied by the courts to both private and public means of control. Zoning is tested in terms of "reasonableness" and so are private restrictions.[13] To summarize briefly, restrictive agreements in deeds are contracts which like all contracts may not be harmful to the public nor contrary to the rational expectations of an average man.

Having considered the legal basis of restrictions, it is pertinent to inquire into some of the mechanics of their structure. Of primary importance is consideration of the difference between a restrictive covenant and a condition.

In spite of a statement by a California court that "the distinction between conditions and covenants is a decided one and the principles applicable quite different,"[14] the loose use of the terms warrants an examination of their respective definitions.

One distinction between a covenant and a condition, often mentioned in the literature of the law, is that the latter impairs the estate conveyed whereas the former does not affect the estate. But from the economic standpoint both covenants and conditions appear designed to prevent certain acts which would impair the interest conveyed or assure performance of certain acts. If a purchaser covenants not to erect a garage and use it for a residence before building the main house, his rights to use the land are lessened, sometimes to his disadvantage. Without going so far as to say that there may not be some cases in which the impairment of legal interests or estates is a distinguishing factor, the chief difference between a covenant and a condition is the remedies available in case of breach. Restrictive covenants will be enforced in equity. An injunction to prevent the violation of the restriction in question is the usual relief sought. The question of damages is a secondary alternative, because the amount of damages is difficult to ascertain for land. Sometimes damages are awarded by the court when an injunction, if issued, would work undue hardship.[15]

The particular kind of conditions with which deed restrictions are concerned is the "condition subsequent." A condition subsequent in a deed provides that the estate is conveyed contingent upon the happening or non-happening of a certain event or upon the performance or non-performance of certain acts. Stated more technically, "subsequent conditions are those whose effect is not produced until after the vesting of the estate or bequest or the commencement of the obligation."[16] Violation of a condition subsequent, on the other hand, may be remedied through a court of law by re-entry of the property.[17] The effect of a condition subsequent is, of course, to make the title rest less securely in the grantee.

[13] "Restrictions will be upheld by the courts provided they are reasonable." *Schoonmaker v. Heckscher*, *supra* n. 7.

[14] *Los Angeles Investment Co. v. Gary*, *supra* n. 2.

[15] See *Page v. Murray*, 46 N. J. Eq. 325 (1890); *Zipp v. Barker*, 55 N. Y. Supp. 246 (1898); *Jackson v. Stevenson*, 156 Mass. 496 (1892).

[16] Bouvier's Law Dictionary, *op. cit.*, article on "Condition."

[17] The purposes of the two devices are also quite different. A covenant is drawn primarily for the protection of the property and may "run with the land," thus becoming binding not only upon the grantee but upon subsequent holders as well. In so far as a condition is frequently drawn with the interests of the grantor in view, it may be said to be more in the nature of a personal agreement.

The following quotation summarizes the clear-cut legal distinction between covenants and conditions subsequent.

"A condition subsequent is also to be distinguished from a covenant, a breach of which cannot, in the absence of a statutory provision to the contrary, affect the estate of the convenantor, but gives to the grantor or lessor, with whom the covenant is made, a right of action to recover damages, for breach thereof, or occasionally a right to an injunction or a decree for specific performance, neither of which is given by a condition."[18]

Thus the chief distinction lies in the remedies available. Which of these devices the subdivider should use in a specific instance depends on his purpose. Inasmuch as his business is the disposal of subdivision lots, he might logically reserve conditions subsequent for only those urgent restrictions, violation of which would seriously endanger the development and thus warrant repossession of the property.

Much litigation has arisen as a result of the loose use of the terms. The courts do not look with favor upon anything which tends to destroy or impair an estate in land and hence their hostility to "conditions subsequent" inserted in deeds. Speaking generally, the evolution of the law of real property has been in the direction of facilitating the transfer of real estate, making land transactions more and more comparable to commodity transactions. Therefore, the attitude of the courts is both logical and explainable, for a condition lessens the security of the title conveyed.

As a result the courts will always construe a condition as a covenant wherever possible. The following quotation is representative of the ample authority on this point.

"Whether the provisions of a deed are to be construed as covenants or as conditions must be determined by a construction of the entire instrument. In case of doubt they will be construed as covenants and not as conditions in order to prevent a forfeiture of the estate, and this construction is to be reached regardless of the technical language used by the parties."[19]

Two major considerations guide the courts in determining whether a restriction shall be construed as a covenant or a condition. The first and most important is the intention of the parties as it may be gleaned from careful examination of the entire instrument and the second is the language of the agreement. Frequently the words in the deed restriction do not convey the intention of the parties and for this reason the two elements are considered separately. A New York case[20] states clearly a position which is fairly representative:

"Although the words of the clause in question (under express condition) are apt to describe a condition subsequent reserved by a grantor, we are in nowise obliged to take them literally. In the consideration of what, by the use of these words, was imported into the conveyance, we are at liberty to affix that meaning to them which the general view of the instrument and of the situation of the parties makes manifest. Whether they created a condition, or a covenant, must depend upon what was the intention of the parties; for covenants and conditions may be created by the same words."

Thus, when a condition subsequent is to be created, that intention should be stated beyond question of doubt. Such phrases as "under this express condition" and "provided always" and "these presents are upon the express condition that" are not sufficient for this purpose,[21]

[18] Herbert Thorndike Tiffany, *The Law of Real Property*, (Chicago: Callaghan & Co., 1920), Vol. I, p. 264.

[19] Robert T. Devlin, *Law of Real Property and Deeds*, (Chicago: Callaghan & Co., 1911), Vol. 2, Sec. 970 c., p. 1812. The author cites as a leading case in this connection *Minard v. Delaware, Lackawanna and Western Railroad Co.*, 139 Fed. 60 (1905).

[20] *Post v. Weil*, 115 N. Y. 361 at 369 (1889).

[21] *Koch v. Streuter*, 232 Ill. 594 (1908); *McCusker v. Goode*, 185 Mass., 607 71 N. E. 76 (1904); *Druecker v. McLaughlin*, 235 Ill. 367, 85 N. E. 647 (1908).

however. The courts regard them merely as means of emphasis and not as introducing a new and separate idea which would involve forfeiture of the estate as a penalty for their violation. In order to create a condition subsequent the most satisfactory method seems to be to include a re-entry clause but even this inclusion will not guarantee construction of the restriction by the courts as a condition subsequent. If the spirit of the instrument as a whole or the situation of the parties at the time the agreement was entered into suggests the slightest doubt as to the creation of a condition, the courts will construe the condition as a covenant.

Another important item in what may be called the legal mechanism of deed restrictions has to do with the question of when restrictions may "run with the land." The major tests of covenants running with the land are whether they pertain to the use, the value or the estate conveyed in that land. All of these tests are represented in the following quotation:

> "In order that a covenant may run with the land and bind assignees it must bear intimate relation with and concern to the estates or lands conveyed . . .
>
> "It runs with the land when performance is made a charge upon the land . . . when performance affects the value of the land . . .
>
> "Where land is divided into parcels conveyed to different grantees, a covenant is divided among them and each may sue or be sued on his portion of the covenant."[22]

The benefit of the land conveyed is the purpose of covenants running with the land.[23] This is the legal way of stating the case, but in the last analysis the benefit of the holders of the land would seem to be the aim. When restrictive agreements benefit only the vendor, they are regarded rather as personal covenants, binding only upon the original parties to the contract. Stated somewhat differently, "in the absence of evidence that the restriction was imposed for the benefit of other land, it is construed as a personal covenant merely with the grantor."[24]

With reference to enforcement, the fact that certain restrictions do run with the land is not a basis for general action. Enforcement of such restrictions rests on the theory that they indicate a general plan of improvement and purchasers with notice of the plan may be compelled by suit of any owner of a lot covered by this plan to comply with the covenant made by the subdivider-vendor.[25] This right to enforce passes with the land for the duration of the restriction. As to phraseology, mere statement to the effect that the restrictive covenants will run with the land is not sufficient. The essence of the restriction itself is the determining factor.[26]

Covenants running with the land are perpetuated through the recording process upon which the whole system of land titles and conveyances has rested for many years. The purposes of the recording statutes are to preserve the "muniments" or evidences of title and to give the community notice of all changes in the ownership of property and the circumstances accompanying such change of ownership. The theory underlying the recording acts has been to place on anyone dealing in land the legal obligation of consulting the records and acquainting himself with their contents. In other words, anyone dealing in land is presumed to have knowledge of the

[22] Christopher G. Tiedeman, *The American Law of Real Property*, (St. Louis: Thomas Law Book Co., 1924), 4th ed., Sec. 626.

[23] *Berryman v. Hotel Savoy Co.*, 160 Cal. 559 (1911).

[24] Devlin, *op. cit.*, sec. 990; the author cites in this connection the case of *Skinner v. Shepard*, 130 Mass. 180 (1881); see also *Wood v. Stehrer*, 119 Md. 143, 86 Atl. 128 (1912).

[25] *Wiegman v. Kusel*, 270 Ill. 520 (1915).

[26] See Tiffany, *op. cit.*, Vol. II, p. 1415.

substance and effect of every properly recorded instrument.[27]

Control over land utilization, which is the main concern of this study, is exercised through covenants which are part of the recorded plats or instruments of conveyance. These restrictive covenants therefore become part of the public record and all subsequent holders are bound by their content under the doctrine of constructive notice. The essence of constructive notice is to be found in the following quotation:

"The test is a plain and simple one. It is whether the record, if examined and read by the party dealing with the premises, would be an *actual* notice to him of the original instrument, and of all its parts and provisions. By the policy of the recording acts, such a party is called upon to search the records, and he has a right to rely upon what he finds there entered as a true and complete transscript of any and every instrument affecting the title to the lands with respect to which he is dealing. A record can only be constructive notice, at most, of whatever is contained within itself. Finally, the record will not be notice unless it and the original instrument of which it is a copy correctly and sufficiently describe the premises which are to be affected, and correctly and sufficiently state all other provisions which are material to the rights and interests of subsequent parties. The premises should at least so be described and identified that a subsequent purchaser or encumbrancer would have the means of ascertaining with accuracy what they were . . . The language both of the original and of the record must be such that if a subsequent purchaser or encumbrancer should examine the instrument itself, he would obtain thereby an actual notice of all the rights which were intended to be created or conferred, by it."[28]

This statement ties up the doctrine of constructive notice very definitely with the recording acts. Any part of the public record is thus binding upon subsequent holders, for they are charged with notice of its contents.

This holds true even though the conveyances to these subsequent holders do not actually mention the restriction.[29]

Consideration of the doctrine of notice should not omit some reference to the concept of actual notice. Actual notice is also binding on subsequent purchasers. But a question may easily be raised as to where to draw the line between actual and constructive notice. One writer goes so far as to say that the distinction is relatively unimportant, unless some statute requires actual notice under certain circumstances. The following quotation illustrates this point of view:

"And so the presence of structures upon the property may be sufficient to charge a purchaser with actual notice of an easement upon the property, provided he has actual knowledge of such structures. But if he were to be charged with notice of the easement by reason of the existence of the structures, independently of his having knowledge of them, the notice would be constructive and not actual."[30]

Consideration of notice and its binding effect upon purchasers leads logically to a discussion of the enforcement of deed restrictions. This phase of the subject falls under two heads: What are the methods of enforcing deed restrictions and by whom are they enforceable?

---

[27] *Johnson v. Hess*, 126 Ind. 298 (1890).

[28] John Norton Pomeroy, *Equity Jurisprudence* (San Francisco: Bancroft-Whitney Co., 1901), 2d ed., vol. 2, sec. 654.

[29] *Ewertsen v. Gerstenberg*, 186 Ill. 344 at 349 (1900) ". . . for we are satisfied from the evidence that this plat was referred to and made a part of the partition deed and subsequent conveyances and has been constantly recognized by all the lot owners as a common source of title and that Ewartsen had notice of it and of said restrictions and is now bound by them unless these restrictions have ceased to exist or are no longer enforceable against him or his said lots, in equity, for reasons hereinafter stated. His property was not relieved from their binding force merely because they were not expressly reserved in the conveyance to him, or in others of the deeds in his chain of title." See also *Library Neighborhood Assn. v. Goosen*, 229 Mich. 89 (1924).

[30] Tiffany, *op. cit.*, vol. 2, p. 2246. See also entire sec. 573.

As stated previously, deed restrictions are enforceable by injunction from a court of equity and by re-entry proceedings in a court of law depending on whether the restrictions are covenants or conditions.

Of greater importance is the question of who may enforce these restrictions. The right of enforcement follows the benefited land. Thus restrictions may be classified from the point of view of enforcement under two general headings: (1) restrictions drawn for the benefit of the grantor are enforceable by him and his assigns in possession of the benefited property against any or all grantees; and (2) restrictions drawn to carry out a general plan for development are enforceable by any grantee against any other grantee.

Restrictions of this latter class are most important for this study and many cases might be cited to illustrate the principle of enforcement in such instances—namely, that the holders of the title to the benefited land have the right to enforce the restrictive agreements.[31]

Restrictions in pursuance of a general scheme are binding upon all who take with notice thereof and are enforceable in equity by any one of these purchasers against any other.[32] In other words, it is privity of estate which counts in such cases and not privity of contract. The personal element becomes secondary and the benefited land is all important in the eyes of the law.

In enforcing deed restrictions there are several things which the courts take into consideration in their interpretation of the instruments. These items constitute a miscellaneous group of considerations which can best be treated *en masse* because they are interrelated and overlapping in their operation. In the first place, the natural inhibition of the courts against restrictions must be considered, for the courts tend to look with disfavor on any impediments to the free use of the landowner's property. A Missouri court states the point concisely in the case of *Zinn* v. *Sidler*[33] where it says that "a restrictive covenant lessens the fee and is not favored at law. It should therefore be made manifest in no uncertain manner and not left entirely to implication . . ."

As a corollary to the presumption against restrictions is the inclination of the courts to construe restrictions in favor of free use of the property whereever the slightest doubt exists as to the meaning of the covenant or the intention of the parties. A host of cases[34] might be cited but the opinion of a Pennsylvania court in *Johnson* v. *Jones*[35] sums up the general attitude on this point as follows: ". . . all doubts are to be resolved against the restriction and in favor of the free and unrestricted use of the property."

The intention of the parties to the contract has already been referred to, both in connection with the distinction

[31] *Summers v. Beeler*, 90 Md. 475 (1899); *Judd v. Robinson*, 41 Colo. 222 (1907); *McNeil v. Gary*, 40 App. D. C. 397 (1913); *Godley v. Weisman*, 113 Minn. 1 (1916); *Wright v. Pfrimmer*, 99 Neb. 447 (1916).

[32] See Pomeroy, *op. cit.*, vol. 4, sec. 1693; also *Allen v. City of Detroit*, 167 Mich. 464 (1911).

[33] 268 Mo. 680, at 689 (1916); see also *Wright v. Pfrimmer*, *supra* n. 3 at 451, where the court says: "Restrictive covenants being in derogation of the landowner's free use of his property, one who claims a right to enforce such covenants has the burden of proving that they were made for his benefit;" also *McNichol v. Townsend*, 73 N. J. Eq. 276 (1907); *Sharp v. Ropes*, 110 Mass. 381 (1872); *Anderson v. Stewart*, 285 Ill. 605 (1918).

[34] *Eckhart v. Irons*, 128 Ill. 568 (1889); *Melson v. Ormsby*, 169 Ia. 522 (1915); *Easterbrook v. Hebrew L. Orphan Soc.*, 85 Conn. 289(1912); *Hutchinson v. Ulrich*, 145 Ill. 336 (1893); *Peabody Heights Co. v. Willson*, 82 Md. 186 (1895); *Schoonmaker v. Heckscher*, *supra* n. 8 at 77. *Randall v. Atlanta Adv. Serv.* 159 Ga. 217 (1924); *Curtis v. Rubin*, 244 Ill. 88 (1910).

[35] 244 Pa. St. 386 at 389 (1914).

between a covenant and a condition and immediately above in connection with the construction in favor of free use of the property. The intention of the parties is a controlling factor in the interpretation and enforcement of deed restrictions, as it is in all forms of contract. The rather elaborate procedure by which intention is determined in restrictive clauses is described by the following quotation from an Iowa opinion.

"Therefore courts of equity have recognized the necessity of looking beyond the mere printed restriction, to the parties themselves; the subject matter of the restriction; the conditions as they exist, surrounding the subjeet matter of the restriction; the topography of the country surrounding the place affected by the restriction; the scheme and purpose to accomplish which the restriction was made; and this in order to ascertain the intent of the parties in respect to the property conveyed."[36]

It may be said, therefore, that the intention of the parties is central in the interpretation of deed restrictions and therefore in their enforcement.[37]

The intention of the parties is materially aided by the drawing of restrictions in connection with a plan for the development of an entire tract. This plan shows the basis for the restrictions and pictures what the parties to the contract propose to do. In their decisions the courts frequently comment upon the presence or absence of a general plan for development and their judgment often hinges on this point.[38] The statement has been made that in Ohio, where the attitude of the court seems to be rather unfavorable to restrictions, in seven cases out of eight in the Supreme Court the restrictions were upheld when they applied to the entire tract. In the eighth case the restrictions varied from lot to lot and were rejected.[39] This evidence is in no sense conclusive but it is an interesting sidelight on the importance that attaches to a plan of development as a basis for deed restrictions.

The idea is sometimes advanced that restrictions drawn in connection with a plan for development are in the nature of an easement.[40] Restrictive agreements may be said to constitute a negative easement. Each lot relinquishes some portion of the free use which would normally accrue to its owner and in return benefits from a similar relinquishment by other parcels in the tract. The opinion of a New York court in *Landsberg* v. *Rosenwasser* contains an interesting statement to this effect.

". . . where a single tract is divided into parcels, and the parcels are conveyed by deeds containing similar restrictive covenants pursuant to a uniform plan adopted for the benefit of all, mutual negative easements are created, each parcel becoming a servient and dominant tenement . . ."[41]

However, there are times when, although the intention of the parties is clear, and the plan of development is definite, the courts will refuse to enforce restrictions in deeds. The most important instance is that involved when the character of the district has so changed that the enforcement of the restrictions would work a real hardship to the land-

[36] *Melson v. Ormsby, supra* n. 34 at 530.

[37] *Peabody Heights Co. v. Willson, supra* n. 34; *Post v. Weil, supra* n. 20; *Godley v. Weisman, supra* n. 31; *Schoonmaker v. Heckscher, supra* n. 8.

[38] *Killien v. Goodman*, 229 Mich. 393, at 399 (1924); *Highland Realty Co. v. Groves*, 130 Ky. 374, 113 S. W. 420 (1908); *Wright v. Pfrimmer, supra* n. 31, at 451; *Library Neighborhood Assn. v. Goosen, supra* n. 29.

[39] *Planning Problems*, 1916, Papers and Discussions of the National Conference on City Planning, p. 108–109.

[40] C. P. Berry, *Digest of the Law of Restrictions on the Use of Real Property* (Chicago: Geo. I. Jones, 1915) p. 367.

[41] 124 N. Y. App. Div. 559, at 561, (1908); see also *Curtis v. Rubin, supra* n. 34; *Riverbank Imp. Co. v. Bancroft*, 209 Mass. 217, 95 N. E. 216 (1911); *Henderson v. Champion*, 83 N. J. Eq. 554, 91 Atl. 332 (1914).

owner. For example, a district may be restricted to single-family residences but obviously equity would be endangered if landowners in that area were restricted to the erection of single-family residences after an elevated line had traversed the center of that district. The presence of the elevated line changed the character of the district and a court of equity would not be inclined to enforce strict residential restrictions because such enforcement would not secure the original purposes of the restrictions.[42] In order to decide whether a district has so changed as to render enforcement of deed restrictions inequitable, the courts reason with respect to two points: Will enforcement of the covenants restore the district to the original character which the restrictions were designed to create and preserve; Is the change in the district the result of violation of the restrictions or of other causes in which the restrictive covenants are not involved?[43] In this connection an Iowa court gave a very broad interpretation of its powers in equity when it said:

"Again it has been the holding of this court that specific performance of a building restrictive covenant rests largely in the sound discretion of the court, and relief will be denied if the defendant will be subject to greater hardship or consequences would be inequitable, but pecuniary loss to defendant will not itself alone prevent enforcement."[44]

The decisions of the courts with respect to change in the character of the district are particularly important in conflicts between zoning ordinances and deed restrictions. By the exercise of this discretionary power a court may prevent or sanction transition to a lower use and thus exert a very considerable influence on the development of the city pattern.

Up to this point attention has been focussed on the enforcement of restrictions and their proper construction to insure enforcement. The question naturally presents itself: How may restrictions be set aside? General Nathan William MacChesney has summarized the means by which deed restrictions may be released or extinguished:[45]

1. "By expiration of the specified time limit;
2. By the uniting in one ownership of the land benefited and restricted;
3. By the parties to the restriction agreement releasing each other;
4. By prior violation of the restriction;
5. Where the character of the locality has so changed that the restriction has lost its effectiveness and a court of equity will in its discretion deny relief against its violation."

This list states clearly the methods available for setting aside deed restrictions and requires but little comment. Points 4 and 5 have already been touched upon. The first point is obvious, but the particular problems clustering about this matter of the duration of restrictive covenants will be discussed in greater detail in a later chapter.

A summary of the legal aspects of deed restrictions from the point of view of the subdivider who creates them should

[42] *Columbia College v. Thatcher*, 87 N. Y. 311 (1882); *Kneip v. Schroeder*, 255 Ill. 621 (1912); *Moore v. Curry*, 176 Mich. 456, 142 N. W. 839 (1913); *Leonard v. Hotel Majestic Co.*, 17 N. Y. Misc. 229, 40 N. Y. Supp. 1044 (1896).

[43] *Jackson v. Stevenson, supra* n. 15: "It is evident that the purpose of the restrictions as a whole was to make the locality a suitable one for residences; and that owing to the general growth of the city and the present use of the whole neighborhood for business, this purpose can no longer be accomplished. If all the restrictions imposed in the deeds should be rigidly enforced, it would not restore to the locality the residential character, but would merely lessen the value of every lot for business purposes. It would be oppressive and inequitable to give effect to the restriction; and since the changed condition of the locality has resulted from other causes than their breach, to enforce them in this instance could have no other effect than to harass and injure the defendant, without effecting the purpose for which the restrictions were originally made."

[44] *Melson v. Ormsby, supra* n. 34, at 533 (1915).

[45] *Op. cit.*, p. 589.

emphasize the legal points to be noted most particularly in drafting restrictive agreements. A primary consideration is the antipathy of the courts to any measure which may be an impediment to the free use of land or its free alienation. At the same time, however, the courts do recognize the right of landowners to regulate the use of the land they convey and the law will uphold restrictive agreements provided they meet certain requirements. The most important requirement is that the instrument express clearly and definitely the intention of the parties to the agreement. If this involves making the title hinge upon a condition subsequent, that fact should be so stated that the courts may clearly ascertain it. The other main requirement is that the restrictions be reasonable—in other words, that the stipulations be in harmony with the general interest and in more or less obvious pursuance of a preconceived plan. If the courts can detect a reasonable intention of the parties with respect to the utilization of the land affected, the restrictive covenants are fairly sure of being sustained at law. The limitations which surround the use of the devices have been considered in some detail. They are the result of the efforts of the law to prevent too great control by the overzealous or ill-advised creator of restrictions or by the "dead hand."[46]

In addition, a summary should not omit to call attention once more to the different requirements of the separate states with respect to the form and content of conveyances. The importance of carefully drafting these agreements so that they will accord with the laws of the particular state in which they are to operate cannot be overemphasized.

A summary from the legal point of view should show the trend in the attitude of the courts with reference to deed restrictions. The importance which the courts are attaching to the existence of a general scheme for the development of a large area is very significant. Such a general plan is held to be evidence of a certain mutuality of interest and purpose which is dominant in the development of legal principles. The increasing use of the phrase "equitable easements" to describe these agreements indicates the tendency to emphasize the mutual nature of the restrictions. But this mutuality centers in the *land*. The parties are rather incidental and the land is all-important. Equitable action involving restrictions of this kind rests on the interest in the land rather than on concurrence in an agreement.[47] In other words, an equitable interest as opposed to a legal interest may be the authority for action in the courts.[48] This attitude of the courts amounts almost to a statement that deed restrictions in pursuance of a general scheme constitute automatic control over land development, in the sense that the human agency is not central in their operation. The increasing use of this form of control particularly in new residential subdivisions promises opportunity for the development of other important legal rulings in the future.

From the economic point of view the significance of the legal aspects of deed restrictions is found in their effect on the potentialities of this device for controlling the use of land and the relationships between persons arising out of such use. Although the courts may emphasize the

[46] The phrase, the "dead hand", refers to "concentration of property without fluidity, without being amenable to control" which the law seeks to prevent. Richard T. Ely, *Property and Contract in Their Relation to the Distribution of Wealth*, (New York, Macmillan Co., 1914), p. 455.

[47] Emphasis is being placed on "privity of estate" rather than "privity of contract."

[48] See Pomeroy, *op. cit.*, vol. 4, sec. 1693.

importance of the land itself, as when covenants are said to run with the land, the economist is concerned with the human relations which at various times center on a particular plot of land. To him the effects of judicial interpretations of deed restrictions upon the parties to land bargains are the most important considerations. This brief examination of the legal aspects shows that deed restrictions, if carefully drawn, are a potent form of control. The courts will uphold them, within limits, and persons seeking to protect their investments in land may with some confidence resort to this device.

CHAPTER IV

Restrictive Clauses Concerning Type and Use of Structures and Lot Area

In studying deed restrictions as a form of control the attempt was made to obtain the necessary information from instruments actually in use in developments over the country. Two main sources were used in securing the deed restrictions for the analysis contained in these chapters. Of the 84 deeds considered 55 were obtained from members of the Home Building and Subdividers Division of the National Association of Real Estate Boards and the Chicago Real Estate Board. The data on the other 29 were taken from a charted summary[1] of deed restrictions on properties planned by Olmsted Brothers, of Brookline, Massachusetts; therefore the information is not so complete as for the other 55. However, they afford opportunity for interesting comparisons, particularly in view of the fact that 23 of the 29 Olmsted cases antedate 1920, while the majority of the other group of 55 cover subdivisions developed since that date and in most cases since 1924.

In view of the sources from which the data were obtained, it cannot be said that the restrictions analyzed here are typical of the subdivision business as a whole. The Home Builders and Subdividers Division of the National Association of Real Estate Boards includes in its membership the developers of most of the better-class subdivisions in the country. Likewise those subdividers who have employed landscape architects of national reputation such as Olmsted Brothers are above the average in the business. It should therefore be emphasized at the outset that the concern here is rather with the different types of control and their effectiveness than with the extent of their use.

The material collected is so diverse and so detailed that some method of condensing it seemed desirable. Hence, a series of tables has been prepared to show the differences as well as the similarities between separate sets of deed restrictions. The brevity necessary in making such a table impairs somewhat the accuracy of the statements but this may be balanced by the value to be derived from being able to compare and visualize the wide divergencies in the scope and character of the restrictive sections of the separate deeds.

Restrictions on the Type and Use of Structures

The developer's plan is the starting point for a discussion of restrictions on the type and use of structures, for the subdivider must decide at the outset what variety of uses, if any, he is going to have in his development. If more than one type of use is to be permitted, it is of course advisable to divide the subdivision into carefully defined use districts and for further protection to designate both the uses permitted and those prohibited.

Taking the prohibitions first, the most obvious are the nuisances. The term "nuisance" has a very broad meaning when used in connection with residential areas, for almost any use not strictly residential in character is a nuisance. The lists of nuisances vary widely, including the most obvious items such as

[1] See *Landscape Architecture*, H. V. Hubbard, "Land Subdivision Restrictions" (Oct., 1925).

TABLE I. RESTRICTIONS PERTAINING TO THE TYPE AND USE OF STRUCTURES*

Name of Subdivision and Subdivider and Location	Business or Trade Prohibited	Type of Improvement	Height of Buildings	Approval of Building Plans	Cost of Buildings	Outbuildings	Nuisances Prohibited
Alleghany Furnace, Baker Estates, Altoona, Pa.	Except on specified lots	Single family residence except on specified lots		Required for bldgs. and alteration by seller		Private garage or greenhouse only	Livestock, signs
Ardmore, J. R. Robertson & Co., Chicago, Ill.		Residences only except on specified lots			$5,000 minimum	Garages must be within 10 ft. of rear of house	
Arlington Park, Laudermilk Realty Co., Chicago, Ill.					Diff. on diff. lots		
Armour Hills, J. C. Nichols Inv. Co., Kansas City, Mo.		Single family residences only			Specified on certain lots.	Correspond to house in style. 35 ft. from lot lines	Fuel tanks above ground
Anchorage Heights, Anchorage, Ky.	Yes	Single family residence only	2 stories, basement		$3,000 minimum		Livestock
Ashburton, G. R. Morris Org'n., Baltimore, Md.	Yes	One dwelling per lot; only 2 story apartment		Required by seller for bldgs. and alterations		Garages only	Fowl
Andrews Subdivision, New Britain, Conn.	Yes	Single family and 2 flat residences	2 stories, basement, attic		$3,000 single $5,000 double		Livestock
Avon Center Estates, H. F. Bowse, Cleveland, Ohio		Single family residences only			$3,000 minimum	Garage min. $200 corresp. to house and built after	Amusement places, liquor
Aspinwall Hill Subd'n, Brookline, Mass.	Yes	Dwellings			$6,000 minimum		
Belmont Country Club, A. T. Mc Intosh Co., Chicago, Ill.					$5,000 on certain lots		
Barton Hills, Ann Arbor, Mich.		Single family residences		Required by maintenance corporation		2 garages combined	Cemetery, livestock
Best Manor, Fred T. Wood Co., Oakland, Cal.	Yes	Single family residences to 1950		Required by seller for bldgs. and alterations	Specified for each lot	Private garage only; erected after house	Livestock, signs
Beacon Falls Rubber Co., Beacon Falls, Conn.	Yes	Single family residences					
Bonelli-Adams Co., Boston, Mass.		Single family residences			$5,000 minimum		
Bonnycastle Terrace, Louisville, Ky.	Yes	Single family residences only					Livestock quarrying, saloon
Brown Section, Thorpe Bros., Minneapolis, Minn.		Single family residences only; 18 exceptions		Required by seller until 1944	Diff. on diff. lots	Private appurtenant only; correspond to house	Fuel tank above ground
Brookline Hills Subd'n, Brookline, Mass.	Yes	Single family residences	3 stories		$4,000		
Cuyahoga View Heights, Hoiles & Hedden Co., Cuyahoga Falls, Ohio	Except on specified lots	Single family residences only; except on some lots	2½ stories maximum	Required by seller for buildings and alterations for 15 yrs.	Diff. on diff. lots	One private garage corresponding to house	Oil well
Colony Hills, Springfield, Mass.	Approved business allowed	Single family residences		Required by trustees		Private garage	Special list

*Another interesting restriction is that which requires the buyer to build on the lot within a certain time after purchase (see p. 33). Such a provision is found in the deeds of the following subdivisions: Ardmore, 1 year on specified lots; Cushing's Island, 2 years; Lake Wauconda, 1 year; Newton Blvd. Sub'n., 2 years; Sackett Sub'n., 5 years; Sudbrook, 5 years.

TABLE I. RESTRICTIONS PERTAINING TO THE TYPE AND USE OF STRUCTURES (*Continued*)

Name of Subdivision and Subdivider and Location	Business or Trade Prohibited	Type of Improvement	Height of Buildings	Approval of Building Plans	Cost of Buildings	Outbuildings	Nuisances Prohibited
Cityco Realty Co.......... Baltimore, Md.	Business prohibited for 10 yrs.				$3,000	Private garage only	Mfr. livestock
Cravath Subdivision........ Locust Valley, L. I.	Yes	Single family residences				Appurtenant to country estate	
Cushing's Island............ Casco Bay, Me.					$2,000		Saloons, Amusements
Deven Heights............ Hogle & Mawdsley Carmel, Cal.	Yes	Single family residence; one per lot		Required by seller			
Devonshire Manor Annex.... Krenn & Dato, Inc. Chicago, Ill.	Manufacturing prohibited	Apartments and business on specified lots		Required by seller; brick, stone or tile		Garages may not be used for residence	Livestock, asylum, etc.
Devonshire Manor.......... Krenn & Dato, Inc. Chicago, Ill.	Business allowed on certain lots	Diff. on diff. lots	Diff. for diff. bldgs.	Required by seller to 1940; brick, tile or stone required	$8,000 for single res.	Garages may not be used for residences to 1950	Livestock, asylum, etc. to 1950
Diana Gardens............ S. S. Berry Chicago, Ill.		Single family residences on all but specified lots			$5,000 single res.		
Estudillo Estates........... Fred T. Wood Co. Oakland, Cal.	Prohibited	Single family residence to 1950		Required by seller for bldgs. and alterations	Diff. for diff. lots	Priv. garage and appurtenant bldgs. Not for res.	Livestock, hospital, etc.
Fairview Addition.......... Chas. P. Gray Chicago, Ill.	Business on specified lots	Single family residences except on specified lots			$6,000 for residences	Garage to be built only in conjunction with res.	
Fairway Section............ Thorpe Bros. Minneapolis, Minn.		Single family residences	1½ story min.	Required by seller for bldgs. and alterations	Diff. for diff. lots	Correspond to residence	Livestock, fuel tank above ground
Forest Hills Gardens........ Sage Foundation Homes Long Island		Private res. for not more than 2 families		Required by seller for bldgs. and alterations	Diff. for diff. lots	Private garage	Slaughter house, livestock
Fernside.................. Fred T. Wood Co. Oakland, Cal.	Business on specified lots	Single family residences	1½ story min.	Required by seller for bldgs. and alterations	Diff. for diff. lots		Livestock, asylum, factory
Freeman Subdivision........ Providence, R. I.	Yes	Single family residences				Garage connected with house recommended	
Gatewood Gardens.......... R. C. Erskine & Co. Seattle, Wash.		Single family residences to 1935				Private garage appurtenant	
Great Neck Hills........... Great Neck, L. I.	Yes	Single family residences		Required by seller	$3,500 to $5,500	Must conform to residence	Livestock
Glen Oaks................. Guy M. Rush Los Angeles, Cal.		Single family residences only		Required by Homes Assn.	$5,000 minimum	Garage may not be erected before house	Livestock, oil drilling
Guilford.................. Baltimore County, Md.		Private dwellings		Required by seller	Diff. for diff. lots	Garage	Extensive list
Gwin Unit................. Fred T. Wood Co. Oakland, Cal.	Prohibited except on specified lots	One single family residence per lot		Required by seller for bldgs. and alterations	$3,000	Private appurtenant; not to be used as res.	
Harroun Park Subdivision... Currier Inv. Co. Detroit, Mich.	Business on specified lots	Single family residences on certain streets			$3,500 to $4,500	Private appurtenant; erected after house	Liquor Mfr. Signs
Highland Park Addition..... Krenn & Dato, Inc. Chicago, Ill.		Single family residences only		Required by seller to 1960 for bldgs. and alterations	$10,000	Garage may not be used as residence	

TABLE I. RESTRICTIONS PERTAINING TO THE TYPE AND USE OF STRUCTURES (*Continued*)

Name of Subdivision and Subdivider and Location	Business or Trade Prohibited	Type of Improvement	Height of Buildings	Approval of Building Plans	Cost of Buildings	Outbuildings	Nuisances Prohibited
Howard-Lincoln, etc., Add'n. Krenn & Dato, Inc. Chicago, Ill.	Business on specified lots	Apartments on specified lots		Required by seller; brick, stone or tile		Garage may not be used as residence	Livestock, hospital, etc.
Hunting Ridge............ Geo. R. Morris Org'n. Baltimore, Md.	Yes	One dwelling per lot; only 2 story apartments		Required by seller for bldgs. and apartments			Fowl, hospital, etc.
Indian Hill Estates......... Bills Realty Co. Chicago, Ill.		Single family residence only	2 story minimum	Required by seller	Diff. on diff. lots		
Kenilworth Hghlds. Subd'n... Wittbold Realty Co. Chicago, Ill.							Mfr. Livestock Billboards
A. H. Kraus Co............ Chicago, Ill.					Diff. on diff. lots	In connection with residence	Signs
Lake Wauconda........... Perry Park, Colo.		Dwellings	30 ft. from ground	Required by seller	$1,500 to $1,000		Liquor
Laudermilk Villa........... B. H. Laudermilk Co. Chicago, Ill.					$8,500 to $10,000		
Lake Shore Highlands....... Oakland, Cal.		Single family residence		Required by seller	$3,000 to $5,000		Special list
Locust Hills............... Blair Homes Co. Altoona, Pa.		One single family residence per lot			$3,000 minimum	Private greenhouse and garage	Livestock billboards
Licton Springs Park......... Seattle, Wash.		Single family residence	2 stories, attic, cellar		$5,000 minimum		Saloon, Factory Hospital
Maple Hill................. F. B. McKibbin Co. Lansing, Mich.		Single family residence		Required by seller	Diff. for diff. lots	Private garage	Liquor, Livestock
Manito Park............... Spokane, Wash.	Yes	Single family residence			$7,500	Conform to house	No quarry
Justin Matthews........... Little Rock, Ark.	Business prohibited	Single family residence—one per lot			Diff. for diff. lots	3 ft. from rear line	Billboards
Milwaukee-Howard, Subd'n.. Krenn & Dato, Inc. Chicago, Ill.	Yes, except on specified lots	Apartments on specified lots		Required by seller; brick, stone or tile		Garage may not be used for residence	Hospital, Livestock
Mountain Lake............ Lake Wales, Florida	Yes	Single family residence		Required by seller			
Morningside Heights........ R. C. Erskine & Co. Seattle, Wash.		Single family residence				Private appurtenant	
Newton Blvd. Subd'n....... Newton, Mass.	Yes	Single family residence	3 stories		$5,000		Livestock
Oak Hill Village............ Arnold Hartman Boston, Mass.	Yes	Single family residence		Required by seller	$12,500 minimum	Private appurtenant	Signs
Oyster Harbor, Inc.......... F. W. Norris Co. Boston, Mass.	Yes	Single family residence	3 stories max.	Required by seller		Private appurtenant	
Pacific Southwest Bank...... Los Angeles, Cal.	Business on specified lots	Diff. on diff. lots			Diff. for diff. uses		Liquor, Signs
Palos Verdes Estates........ Los Angeles, Cal.	Business on specified lots	Single family residence		Required by Art Jury & Homes Assn.	Diff. for diff. lots		Signs, Factories, Oil drills
Redmont Park............ Jemison & Co. Birmingham, Ala.	Yes	Single family residence		Required by seller	$10,000 minimum	Usually attached; private appurtenant	

TABLE I. RESTRICTIONS PERTAINING TO THE TYPE AND USE OF STRUCTURES (*Continued*)

Name of Subdivision and Subdivider and Location	Business or Trade Prohibited	Type of Improvement	Height of Build-ings	Approval of Building Plans	Cost of Build-ings	Outbuildings	Nuisances Pro-hibited
Roland Park............... Baltimore County, Md.	Business prohibited	Dwellings			Diff. for diff. lots		Livestock
St. Frances Wood.......... Mason-McDuffie Co. San Francisco, Cal.	Yes	Private dwelling house	2 sto-ries max.	Required by Homes Ass'n	$4,000 mini-mum	Private appurte-nant; not built before house	Liquor Livestock, Factory
Sackett Subdivision......... Louisville, Ky.							
Scarsdale Estates........... New York City	Yes	One dwelling house per lot; no apt. or duplex		Required by seller to 1935	Diff. for diff. lots	Garage appur-tenant	Saloon, Factory
Sudbrook.................. Baltimore County, Md.	Yes	Single family residence	3 sto-ries		$3,000		Livestock
Shaker Heights............. Van Sweringen Co. Cleveland, Ohio		One single fam-ily residence per lot	2 sto-ries min.	Required by seller		Private garage; conforming to house	
Sunalta.................... Calgary, Alberta	Yes				$500 to $2,000		
S. Bloomfield Highlands..... Michigan Inv. Co. Detroit, Mich.		Single family residence	Related to foun-dation	Required by seller; brick or stone material		Private appur-tenant	
Sunrise Addition............ R. C. Erskine & Co. Seattle, Wash.		Single family residence			Diff. for diff. lots	Private garage appurtenant	
Sunnymede................ Whitcomb & Keller S. Bend, Ind.				Required by seller for bldg. and alterations		Garage not to be erected before house	Livestock
Sunnyside City Housing Corp. New York City							
Tavern Acres.............. N. Andover, Mass.	Yes	Single family residence			$6,500		Livestock, Signs
Tilden Realty Corp. .... Utica, N. Y.		Single family residence			$14,000 $10,000 $5,000	Garage	
Sunset Hill................. J. C. Nichols Inv. Co. Kansas City, Mo.		Single family residence		Stated in individ-ual deeds or con-tracts	Diff. for diff. lots		
Uplands.................. Victoria, B. C.	Yes	Dwellings	2 sto-ries		$5,000		Saloon, Livestock, Signs
Uplands.................. Wellesley, Mass.	Yes	Single family residence			$7,500	Garage; conser-vatory	Livestock, Signs
Valencia Park.............. Bowie & Trent San Benito, Tex.	Yes, except on specified lots	Single family residence			$3,500 to $5,000	Private appurte-nant; may not be used for res.	
Vanderlip Subd'n........... Scarborough, N. Y.		Single family residence	2 sto-ries		$10,000 $15,000 $20,000		Special list
Vinsetta Park Subd'n........ Vinsetta Land Co. Detroit, Mich.	Business on specified lots	One dwelling; not more than 2 apts.		Required by seller	Diff. on diff. streets		
Wagner-Thoreson Co........ Los Angeles, Cal.		Single family residences except on specified lots			Diff. for diff. uses		Livestock
Woodmar.................. Woodmar Realty Co. Hammond, Ind.	Business on specified lots	Use classification of lots		Required by seller	Speci-fied for each lot	Garages only on residence lots	Mfr. Liquor Billboards
Westchester................ William Zelosky Chicago, Ill.	Business on specified lots	Single family residences; apts. on certain lots		No frame con-struction al-lowed	$5,000	Private appur-tenant	
Westwood Subdivision....... Van Alstine Land Co. Detroit, Mich.	Business on specified lots	Diff. on diff. lots			Diff. for diff. uses	Private appur-tenant; erected after house	

the keeping of chickens, the erection of billboards, fuel tanks above ground, etc., as well as other items not so obviously detrimental to residence use. Manufacturing, as a prohibited use, is frequently found among the list of nuisances, along with hospitals, asylums and other institutional uses. An examination of the lists shows that they reflect local prejudices quite definitely. An example is to be found in the restrictions on properties in northeastern Ohio, where a prohibition against gas and oil drilling is found, as a result of a drilling fever which swept that section about 15 years ago and peppered it with unsightly derricks. It is with a view to meeting local situations such as this that lists of nuisances should be compiled in order to be most effective.

If the subdivision is to be purely residential, a blanket restriction is frequently drawn, prohibiting the use of any structure for purposes of business or trade. Two or three typical restrictions of this character may be cited:

"The party of the second part shall not at any time conduct or permit to be conducted upon said premises any trade or business."[2]

"No building erected or placed thereon shall be used for any business, trade, manufacturing, mercantile or mechanical purposes . . ."[3]

"This property shall be used for residence purposes only and not for any purpose of business or trade."[4]

However, a subdivision may be designed primarily for residential purposes and still include a limited number of business sites. At this point the developer exercises his zoning power by determining how much business area he will set aside and also where it shall be located. A common method of describing both amount and location is by reference to the recorded plat of the subdivision or, in cases where no such recording has taken place, by reference to street frontage. Examples of each of these methods follow.

". . . nor shall any of said property . . . be used for any purpose other than residence purposes, except that Lots Nos. 245 to 253, inclusive, as shown on said Map may be devoted to the purposes and uses specified and permitted for the Class 5 business district provided and established by Ordinance 227 . . ."[5]

"It is mutually agreed that for a period of twenty (20) years from date hereof, that lots facing on Palatine (Central) Road may be used for business purposes, . . ."[6]

Next comes the question of residential uses and whether or not other than single-family residences shall be permitted. In subdivisions which include both single- and multi-family houses the procedure, so far as the restrictions are concerned, is similar to that used in designating business uses and business location. The deed will refer to the recorded plat or specify certain streets for the location of multi-family units. When a variety of uses is allowed, subdividers are usually quite careful in their terminology, specifying apartment use, two-family, or three-family buildings. The mere fact of having to distinguish between two or more types of use makes clear-cut terminology necessary.

But when it is desired to set aside an area for single-family residences a wide variety of terms is used, frequently resulting in difficulties. The term "dwelling," for example, is often used but it may be construed to mean a single building which may house more than one family quite as easily as to mean a single-family residence which was probably the subdivider's intention. Likewise the terms "family residence" and "residen-

[2] Deven Heights, Hogle & Mawdsley, Carmel, Cal.
[3] Oak Hill Village, Arnold Hartman, Boston, Mass.
[4] Redmont Park, Jemison & Co., Birmingham, Ala.
[5] Fernside, Fred T. Wood Co., Oakland, Cal.
[6] Fairview Addition, Chas. P. Gray Co., Chicago, Ill.

tial purposes" are liable to misconstruction. It therefore behooves the subdivider to take great pains in phrasing the clause which designates certain lots for single-family residence use. A particularly good statement of this restriction is found in covenants for the Armour Hills property of the J. C. Nichols Investment Co. of Kansas City:

"None of said lots may be improved, used or occupied for other than private residence purposes, and no flat nor apartment house, though intended for residence purposes may be erected thereon. Any residence erected or maintained thereon shall be designed for occupancy by a single family."

Such a statement as this is sometimes further strengthened by an addition to the effect that only one such residence shall be placed on a lot.[7]

Finally, consideration of the type and use of structures must include the regulations with respect to outbuildings: What kinds shall be permitted, to what uses may they be put, by whom may they be used and when shall they be built? Although occasional mention is made of greenhouses, garages are the most important form of outbuildings and most restrictions are concerned with their regulation. Most of the restrictions state that private garages, for use only by occupants of the house, may be built, with occasional reference to capacity, as two- or three-car garages. Some restrictions state that the garage shall conform to the type of architecture of the house and shall be attached to the house or located on the lot with special reference to the house or building lines. Another very important group of regulations consists of those which stipulate when the garage shall be built or for what it shall be used. An increasingly common restriction states that the garage shall not be built before the house and/or that the garage shall not be used for residential purposes.

"No accessory building or outhouse of any kind shall be erected and maintained on any lot prior to the erection of the main residence thereon."[8]

"No garage, barn or other outbuilding, erected on said lot, shall at any time be used for residential purposes."[9]

Restrictions of this type have grown up to meet a situation of fairly recent origin in which lot purchasers have bought the land, erected a garage and used it for a residence while accumulating funds for the construction of the house. The chief difficulty which may arise as a result of failure to include such a restriction as this is the construction of buildings of this type before the completion of improvements. Prevention of such contingencies is obviously desirable. From the point of view of selling the balance of the lots in a subdivision the erection of garage-residences is a distinct handicap in the development of a high-class subdivision. On the other hand, in a subdivision designed for lower income groups permission to erect such structures may be an aid in disposing of remaining lots. In such instances the number of prospective purchasers will be increased because they will not have to wait to acquire funds for both house and lot before purchasing.

After planning for the types of structures and the uses to which they may be put, the developer proceeds to regulate the construction of these buildings. An occasional restriction stipulates that building shall be started within a specified time after the purchase of the land. The purpose of this restriction is obvi-

[7] "Only one single family residence shall be erected on each individual lot." (Locust Hills, Blair Homes Co., Altoona, Pa.)

[8] Glen Oaks, Guy M. Rush, Los Angeles, Cal.

[9] Milwaukee-Howard-Harlem-Subdivision, Krenn & Dato, Chicago, Ill.

ously to insure improvement of the area within a relatively short time. This would, of course, redound to the benefit of the subdivider, for it is easier to sell the remaining lots in a subdivision when construction and utilization are under way. Only one such restriction is found among the 55 subdivisions which are the most recent developments and of the five such restrictions in the 29 Olmsted subdivisions none are found later than 1917. Furthermore, the one recent subdivision does not make a blanket restriction requiring construction to take place within a certain time on all lots. Instead this subdivider has reserved certain lots which may be sold only to purchasers who agree to build within one year.[10] An examination of the plat reveals that the lots so reserved are scattered over the subdivision, their locations being determined probably by the fact that buildings erected on these sites would be strategic from the point of view of inducing further building. It would be interesting to know whether any concessions were made in the prices of these lots to compensate for the additional restriction. This restriction is an attempt on the part of the subdivider to have lot purchasers share with him the responsibility of pioneering in the new development. But the general attitude of regarding this as a responsibility primarily of the subdivider may explain in part the very few instances of this type of control.

The inference to be derived from the disappearance of this restriction is that it retarded too much the sale of lots. The question might be raised as to whether greater use of this device might not be desirable to curb the speculative character of land sales. The insertion of a time limit for building indicates sale for use and not for speculation. It protects the lot purchaser who wishes to build promptly from a long period of pioneering. In other words, the man who builds as soon as the subdivision is opened often has to wait several years before enough other structures are built in the area to give him any of the advantages of a community development. The time limit on building would benefit the consumers of this class. The immediateness of improvement has long been the stock argument of the subdivision salesman. Such a restriction writes this statement of the salesman into the contract. It thus becomes binding upon all the lot purchasers who thus secure for themselves the advantages derived from prompt building.

By far the most important restriction upon construction is that which requires the approval of building plans. A statement in a report by Olmsted Brothers sums up the case for the approval of building plans.

> "Of all the restrictions that have been devised to regulate or limit the uses of land for the purpose of maintaining high average values in a community, one of the most important, certainly the most broadly inclusive, and when skillfully employed the most effective, is a reservation to the vendor development company, or to some other agency acting for the common benefit of all property owners, of the power to veto the execution of plans for improvements which in the opinion of that agency would detrimentally affect the attractiveness and consequent land values of the neighborhood for the general purposes which may have been chosen as appealing most strongly to the market to which the development is intended to cater."[11]

The importance of the restriction is further attested by the fact that 39, or almost half, of the 84 deeds analyzed contain such clauses. It should be noted, however, that this high percentage may

[10] Ardmore, John R. Robertson & Co., Chicago, Ill.

[11] "Restrictions for Residential Subdivisions,' p. 3 (1925).

be the result in large part of the nature of the sources from which these restrictions were collected. Further examination of the facts reveals an interesting trend. Thirty-two of the 55 more recent deeds contain a requirement for approval of building plans, whereas only seven of the 29 in the Olmsted group contain such clauses, all of which are dated since 1908. In other words, in so far as any generalization may be made from so small a sample, it may be said that this device is comparatively new and that its use is increasing.

The best of these restrictions are quite inclusive. They cover approval not only of the original structures but also of alterations thereto. A typical clause runs as follows:

"No building, fence, wall or other structure shall be commenced, erected or maintained, nor shall any addition to or change or alteration therein be made, until the plans and specifications, showing the nature, kind, shape, height, materials, floor plans, color scheme, location and approximate cost of such structure and the grading of the plot to be built upon shall have been submitted to and approved by Whitcomb and Keller, and a copy thereof, as finally approved, lodged permanently with Whitcomb and Keller. Whitcomb and Keller shall have the right to refuse to approve any such plans or specifications or grading plan, which are not suitable or desirable, in its opinion, for aesthetic or other reasons; and in so passing upon such plans, specifications and grading plans, it shall have the right to take into consideration the suitability of the proposed building or other structure, and of the materials of which it is to be built, to the site upon which it is proposed to erect the same, the harmony thereof with the surroundings and the effect of the building or other structure as planned, on the outlook from the adjacent or neighboring property. A landscape development plan shall be submitted to and approved by Whitcomb and Keller before any landscaping is actually executed."[12]

Harmonious development is obviously promoted if these powers are carefully administered.

From the point of view of the purchaser two considerations should be noted. There is valuable sales psychology in this restriction. Each individual purchaser is prone to feel that his own taste in residence design is quite unimpeachable, but he is not so sure about his neighbor. The existence of this restriction assures him that his neighbor will not erect an architectural atrocity which will lessen the amenities of his own improvement.

The second concern of the purchaser is a corollary of this. It has to do with the purchaser's confidence in the subdivider with respect to performing the duties placed upon him by this restriction. The success of this restriction is dependent upon the performance of the subdivider or of the agent whom he has charged with the administration of this covenant. If high standards are maintained in the early improvements, the sale of the last lots will be materially aided. If, on the other hand, the restriction is loosely administered, it will destroy confidence in the subdivider and although his immediate sales may be speeded up by the lowering of the standards, he will lose the clientele to which he was appealing originally.

An important consideration in connection with this restriction is the agency for administering it. If there is confidence in the subdivider then administration by him is the easiest way to handle the problem. However, his interest is apt to lag as the lots are sold out and in order to get out more quickly, he may be tempted to lower his standards toward the end.

Administration by an association of the lot owners also presents difficulties. Although this may be a sales asset, it is difficult to handle, particularly in the

[12] Sunnymede, Whitcomb & Keller, South Bend, Ind.

early stages of the development. On the other hand, if such an association is not formed until the lots are nearly disposed of, the subdivider may again let down the bars before withdrawing in favor of the owners' association.

The third alternative for administering this restriction is by an Art Jury. The chief problem is to secure an adequate personnel for such a body and this is especially difficult when the subdivision is not near a large city.

Another administrative problem has to do with the cost involved in approving plans. The approval of a large number of building plans involves considerable outlay. Olmsted Brothers in their report have suggested that a fee be charged for such approval. This would be particularly useful when the subdivider's interest begins to decline and he cannot be expected to bear the financial burden involved. It is also a desirable expedient if the administration is in the hands of an owners' association, for such an organization has no funds out of which to meet such expenses.

This matter of approval of building plans is being approached from a different angle. The development of architectural control as it has been worked out on the Palos Verdes Estates in California is the outstanding example. Since the broad outlines of this method were traced in Chapter II, the additional discussion here is intended only to show the wide scope of this control. The purpose is not to require the use of a particular style of architecture but rather to encourage the development of a style suited to California conditions. In order to secure harmony within a given district the height of the roof has been the determining factor. In other words, three different residence districts are described in terms of high roof, medium roof, or low roof. This constitutes rather a far-reaching measure of control but it seems to be successful.

Although no court cases have arisen to test this control, certain decisions are considered to pave the way for a favorable verdict. Proponents of architectural control base their confidence in its legality largely on the fact that restrictions requiring approval of building plans have been sustained in some courts. A leading Maryland case is usually quoted on this point:

> "The second part of the by-law provides that the design of the building shall be approved by the directors. The object of this provision . . . was to secure the erection of a better class of buildings with attractive surroundings, and to prevent the erection of inferior buildings that might diminish the value of the property and affect its eligibility for building purposes. It was intended not only for the benefit of the lessor and the company, but for the common advantage and protection of all persons coming in or taking title under the company . . . And in addition to this we may add, that it is perfectly competent for the company in selling or leasing the property, to provide in the lease or conveyance or by agreement, for the erection of buildings according to a certain designated plan or design . . . So the only objection that the defendant can fairly make to the title offered by the company is the restriction which requires the design of the building to be erected by him to be submitted for the approval of the directors . . . The general rule deducible from the authorities seems to be that where the intention of the parties is clear, and the restrictions within reasonable bounds, they will be upheld. In our opinion the covenant involved in this case meets these tests."[13]

Other more recent decisions[14] likewise uphold the validity of restrictions requiring approval of building plans. It remains for actual experience to prove whether a defense based on these

[13] *Peabody Heights Co. v. Willson*, 82 Md. 186 at 202, 203 and 204 (1895).

[14] *Harmon v. Burow*, 262 Pa. 188 (1919); *Jones v. Northwest Real Estate Co.*, 149 Md. 271, 131 Atl. 446 (1925).

grounds will result in judicial approval of architectural control as it has been developed in California.

A comparison of the two forms of control—the approval of building plans and architectural control—raises several interesting questions. The approval of building plans is open to the danger of arbitrary administration, for it gives very wide powers to the enforcing agency. On the other hand, if carefully administered, it offers an opportunity for a greater variety of building construction while retaining a harmonious and pleasing general effect. Architectural control would seem to afford somewhat less elasticity in design. But from the point of view of the powers conferred it appears less drastic, in that it requires the establishment and publication of certain standards of construction which may be definitely known by the prospective purchaser of a lot.

Economically either method of control must be tested in the light of its effect upon land values. The problem in drafting such restrictions is to strike the proper balance between control which will stabilize values and control which will constitute an interference with, and thus an impairment of, values.

Two other restrictions sometimes applied to the construction of residences deserve attention. One is a stipulation as to the height of the building; sometimes expressed in feet, sometimes in the number of stories. The need for this restriction may be questioned in cases where the approval of building plans is required. But it is not uncommon to find both types of restrictions in the same deed.

The other restriction to be considered is that which stipulates the minimum cost of the buildings to be erected on the subdivision. Two methods are employed in applying this restriction; a blanket minimum may be set for all residences to be built in the subdivision or a schedule may be prepared setting forth specific minimum costs for each lot or block of lots. Of these two methods the second is clearly the better, for there are but few subdivisions in which all lots warrant equal treatment as to the improvements to be erected on them. The value of a restriction in terms of minimum cost may be questioned. The main argument in its favor is that such a restriction may be valuable from the point of view of advertising and sales psychology. This will depend upon the local market conditions. On the other side, proponents of a minimum cost of building clause must answer the question: Is this an effective device for enforcing the developer's plan? In the first place, it is very difficult to determine the actual value of a structure in dollars. Furthermore, such a restriction does not insure an attractive or harmonious improvement. A lot purchaser may comply with or even exceed the minimum cost set by the agreement and yet his residence may be a positive blot on the subdivision. Another obstacle to the usefulness of this stipulation is the changing value of the dollar, which may make a $5,000 minimum, for example, totally inadequate to provide a desirable improvement in harmony with the plan for the development. In a subdivision which is quickly sold out and built up a stipulation as to the cost of improvement may be workable but it is of doubtful value in a slow development. Finally, this restriction is of minor significance when approval of building plans is required.

Restrictions on Use of the Lot Area

When deeds contain only a very limited number of restrictive clauses, setback provisions are almost invariably among the regulations included. Building lines are by far the most important of the restrictions pertaining to the use of the lot area. Probably they are likewise the most difficult to draft. There are two principal ways of establishing these lines. One is by drafting or writing them in the plat of the subdivision which is filed in the office of the county recorder. The other is to insert them in the deeds conveying the property. The former procedure needs no proof to show that such restrictions are part of a general scheme for the development of the area. They are enforceable by and against all grantees of the subdivider, and are binding upon subsequent purchasers with notice, even though they are not mentioned in the conveyances.

It is somewhat more difficult, however, to show beyond question of a doubt that building lines established by restrictive clauses in deeds are in pursuance of a general scheme. Special care must therefore be exercised in framing these agreements to prove that their purpose is to promote a balanced plan for the entire development. But in spite of this possible difficulty the method of establishing building lines by clauses in the instruments conveying the property seems preferable. It permits more careful definition, particularly in subdivisions where the developer has taken pains to work out his general scheme in terms of the requirements for each lot. When such building line clauses are part of a general scheme, they may be enforced by all grantees of the subdivider.[15]

The two main elements in building lines are the front building line and the side building line. The front line is important, of course, because of its relation to the general appearance of the subdivision. The side building line, while also contributing to the amenities of the layout, is more important from the point of view of securing adequate light and air for the individual lot owners. The differences in purpose of the two types are reflected in the terminology which is sometimes used to describe them. The front building line is frequently referred to as the setback line while the side building lines are often treated under the heading of "free spaces." The front building line should be platted with reference to topography and particularly to street plan, for setback restrictions on lots fronting on a major thoroughfare may well be greater than on lots fronting on minor streets. The side building lines are determined largely by the lot width, which in turn is determined by land values and general character of the development. Their main purpose is to prevent building too far to one side of the lot or too close to the adjoining residences.

Another classification of building line restrictions may be made with reference to their inclusiveness or the care with which they are drawn. Three groups may be distinguished. The first is composed of blanket restrictions which establish a single building line for all lots. The second group consists of restrictive clauses which designate front and side building lines with occasional reference to projections. The third classification includes those restrictions which establish building lines for each lot separately.

An example of restrictions of the first class is one which establishes a "20-foot building line on all residential lots."[16] Such a procedure suggests several difficulties. In the first place, it ignores completely any topographical irregularities. Furthermore, it makes no provision for questions which will inevitably arise, such as: May the lower step rest

[15] *Van Sant v. Rose*, 260 Ill. 401 (1913).

[16] Arlington Park, *B.* H. Laudermilk Realty Association, Chicago, Illinois.

TABLE II. RESTRICTIONS PERTAINING TO THE USE OF THE LOT AREA*

Name of Subdivision and Subdivider and Location	Building Lines	Projections	Lot Frontage	Percent. of Lot Area Covered	Further Subdivision	Public Areas	Easements
Alleghany Furnace.......... Baker Estates Altoona, Pa.	Recorded on plat	5 ft. beyond bldg. line for enclosed porch		80% lot width	Prohibited		5 ft. rear 3 ft. side
Ardmore.................. J. R. Robertson & Co. Chicago, Ill.	25 ft. on all lots						
Arlington Park............ Laudermilk Realty Co. Chicago, Ill.	20 ft. on all residence lots						
Armour Hills.............. J. C. Nichols Inv. Co. Kansas City, Mo.	Recorded on plat	Diff. amts. for diff. types of projections	45 ft. min. on spec. sts.	80% lot width			
Anchorage Heights.......... Anchorage, Ky.	Main walls 10 ft. from side and rear lines. 100 ft. from street	Diff. amts. for diff. types of projections			Prohibited	Title reserved by seller	
Ashburton................ G. R. Morris Org'n Baltimore, Md.			50 ft. minimum				
Andrews Sub'n............ New Britain, Conn.					Only with consent of seller		5 ft. side or rear
Avon Center Estates........ H. F. Bowse Cleveland, Ohio	30 ft. front, 3–8 ft. side depending on drive						
Aspinwall Hill Sub'n........ Brookline, Mass.						Title reserved by seller	
Belmont Country Club...... A. T. Mc Intosh Co. Chicago, Ill.	35 ft. building line on all but specified lots						On record
Barton Hills............... Ann Arbor, Mich.	Main walls 25 ft. from street. 10 ft.–20 ft. from side and rear					Title reserved by seller	
Best Manor................ Fred T. Wood Co. Oakland, Cal.	Specified for each lot						
Beacon Falls.............. Beacon Falls, Conn.	Main walls 15 ft. from streets						
Bonelli-Adams Co........... Boston, Mass.	25–50 ft. from street line depending on depth						
Bonnycastle Terrace........ Louisville, Ky.	Main walls 100 ft. from street. 10 ft. from side and rear line	Diff. amts. for diff. types of projections			Prohibited		
Brown Section.............. Minneapolis, Minn. Thorpe Bros.	Main walls 40 ft. from front lot line and 5 ft. from side line	Diff. for diff. types of projections		60% total; 80% width		Riparian rights reserved	
Brookline Hills Sub'n....... Brookline, Mass.	20, 10 ft. from front st.; 5 ft. from side and rear lines	Blanket permission for projections				Reservation of title by seller	
Cuyahoga View Heights..... Hoiles & Hedden Co. Cuyahoga Falls, Ohio	Specified in each deed	Projections require approval of builder			Prohibited		5 ft. rear
Colony Hills.............. Springfield, Mass.	Special schedule. 10 ft. from rear line	Diff. amts. for diff. types of projections	30 ft. minimum free space			Title reseved by seller	
Cityco Realty Co........... Baltimore, Md.	Set-back 30 ft. from street line	Projections may go 8 ft. beyond building line	40 ft. minimum				

*An additional restriction specifying a minimum lot area is found in the deeds of two subdivisions: Sudbrook, 1 house per acre; Sunrise Addition, 4,000 sq. ft.

TABLE II. RESTRICTIONS PERTAINING TO THE USE OF THE LOT AREA (*Continued*)

Name of Subdivision and Subdivider and Location	Building Lines	Projections	Lot Frontage	Percent. of Lot Area Covered	Further Subdi-vision	Public Areas	Ease-ments
Cravath Sub'n. Locust Valley, L. I.	20 ft. from side and front streets				Offer to neighbor before selling	Seller reserves title to marsh	
Cushing's Island. Casco Bay, Me.							
Deven Heights. Hogle & Mawdsley Carmel, Cal.					Prohibited for 25 yrs.		
Devonshire Manor Annex. Krenn & Dato, Inc. Chicago, Ill.	Set-back 15 ft. from street	No projection within 15 ft. of street					Of record
Devonshire Manor. Krenn & Dato, Inc. Chicago, Ill.	Set-back 12 ft. from street	No projection within 12 ft. of street				Seller will improve and maintain to 1930	Of record
Diana Gardens. S. S. Berry Chicago, Ill.							
Estudillo Estates. Fred T. Wood Co. Oakland, Cal.							
Fairview Addition. Chas. P. Gray Co. Chicago, Ill.	Set-back 27 ft. from street	No projections within 27 ft. of street					
Fairway Section. Thorpe Bros. Minneapolis, Minn.	Main walls 35 ft. from front line and 5 ft. from side line	Projections not more than 12 ft. beyond main wall		60% total 80% width			
Forest Hills Gardens. Sage Foundation Homes Long Island	Main walls 25 ft. from front street and 12½ ft. from side	Diff. amts. for diff. types of projections					On map. 3 ft. rear
Fernside. Fred T. Wood Co. Oakland, Cal.	Private garage only	Diff. for diff. lots	40 ft. minimum				On map
Freeman Sub'n. Providence, R. I.	20–12 ft. for main walls						
Gatewood Gardens. R. C. Erskine & Co. Seattle, Wash.	Main front walls 20 ft. from lot line						
Great Neck Hills. Great Neck, L. I.	20–25 ft. main walls from street	12 ft. from side street				Reserved by seller	
Glen Oaks. Guy M. Rush Los Angeles, Cal.	Diff. for diff. lots						5 ft. rear 3 ft. side
Guilford. Baltimore County, Md.	Special schedule	Diff. for diff. types of projections				Reserved by seller	5 ft. rear
Gwin Unit. Fred T. Wood Co. Oakland, Cal.							
Harroun Park Sub'n. Currier Inv. Co. Detroit, Mich.	20–25 ft. set-back from front lot line	Projections may go beyond building line					
Highland Park Addition. Krenn & Dato, Inc. Chicago, Ill.							Of record
Howard-Lincoln etc. Add'n. Krenn & Dato, Inc. Chicago, Ill.	15 ft. set-back from street	15 ft. set-back for projections					Of record
Hunting Ridge. Geo. R. Morris Org'n Baltimore, Md.	Bldg. 10 ft. and garage 3 ft. from party line		50 ft. minimum				
Indian Hill Estates. Bills Realty Co. Chicago, Ill.	50 ft. set-back for main walls	50 ft. set-back for projections					Of record

TABLE II. RESTRICTIONS PERTAINING TO THE USE OF THE LOT AREA (*Continued*)

Name of Subdivision and Subdivider and Location	Building Lines	Projections	Lot Frontage	Percent. of Lot Area Covered	Further Subdivision	Public Areas	Easements
Kenilworth Hghlds. Sub'n... Wittbold Realty Co. Chicago, Ill.							
A. H. Kraus Co. Chicago, Ill.	Of record; diff. for diff. lots	Porches, etc. may project beyond bldg. line					
Lake Wauconda Perry Park, Colo.	Main wall 30 ft. from front street, 5 ft. from side st.					Title reserved by seller	
Laudermilk Villa B. H. Laudermilk Co. Chicago, Ill.	30 ft. on all lots						
Lake Shore Highlands Oakland, Cal.	Special schedule					Title reserved by seller	5 ft. on certain lines
Locust Hills Blair Home Co. Altoona, Pa.	Set-back 18 ft. from street	Porch may project beyond 18 ft.			Prohibited		On plat
Licton Springs Pk. Seattle, Wash.	Main walls 40 ft. from front and side streets	Diff. amts. for diff. types of projections				Title reserved by seller	
Maple Hill F. B. McKibben Co. Lansing, Mich.	Set-back 25 ft. from front and 6 ft. from side lot line				Prohibited		2 ft. rear and side lines
Manito Park Spokane, Wash.	Main walls 35 ft. from front and 5 ft. from side lines						
Justin Matthews Co. Little Rock, Ark.							
Milwaukee-Howard etc. Sub'n Krenn & Dato, Inc. Chicago, Ill.	20 ft. set-back from street	No projections beyond 20 ft.					Of record
Mountain Lake Lake Wales, Fla.	Main walls 10 ft. from side and rear lines					Title reserved by seller	5 ft. north and east
Morningside Heights R. C. Erskine & Co. Seattle, Wash.	Front walls 25 ft. from lot line						
Newton Blvd. Sub'n Newton, Mass.	Main walls 25 ft. from front and 5 ft. from side line	Diff. amts. for diff. types of projections				Title reserved by seller	
Oak Hill Village Arnold Hartman Boston, Mass.	Main walls of house 25 ft. from street line						
Oyster Harbor, Inc. F. W. Norris Co. Boston, Mass.	Set-back 50 ft. from street and 20 ft. from lot line						
Pacific Southwest Bank Los Angeles, Cal.	Set-back 15 ft. from front lot line	Steps may encroach on 15 ft. set-back					
Palos Verdes Estates Los Angeles, Cal.	Diff. for diff. lots			Diff. for diff. uses	Prohibited		
Redmont Park Jemison & Co. Birmingham, Ala.	Diff. for diff. lots						Reserved at rear
Roland Park Baltimore County, Md.	Special schedule						
St. Francis Wood Mason-McDuffie Co. San Francisco, Cal.	Schedule by lots						On map
Sackett Sub'n Louisville, Ky.					Into no more than 4 lots		

TABLE II. RESTRICTIONS PERTAINING TO THE USE OF THE LOT AREA (*Continued*)

Name of Subdivision and Subdivider and Location	Building Lines	Projections	Lot Frontage	Percent. of Lot Area Covered	Further Subdi-vision	Public Areas	Ease-ments
Scarsdale Estates New York City	Diff. for diff. lots						
Sudbrook Baltimore County, Md.	Main walls 40 ft. from front and 10 ft. from side st.	May project 5 ft. into set-back area			Prohib-ited	Title re-served by seller	Reserved
Shaker Heights Van Sweringen Co. Cleveland, Ohio	Schedule for indi-vidual lots				Prohib-ited with-out seller		
Sunalta Calgary, Alberta	Main walls 20 or 30 ft.						
S. Bloomfield Highlands Michigan Inv. Co. Detroit, Mich.	Set-back 50 ft. from street line	Projections may go 12 ft. beyond building line					6 ft. on rear line
Sunrise Addition R. C. Erskine & Co. Seattle, Wash.	20–25 ft. set-back from front lot line			35% in-side and 45% cor-ner lot			
Sunnymede Whitcomb & Keller So. Bend, Ind.	Recorded on plat	Diff. amts. for diff. types of projections			Prohib-ited with-out sell-er's con-sent		
Sunnyside City Housing Corp. New York City							Of record
Tavern Acres N. Andover, Mass.	Main walls 25 ft. from front and 10 ft. from side street				Not to violate re-strictions		
Tilden Realty Corp. Utica, N. Y.	Main walls 50, 100 and 20 ft. from front street				To speci-fied mini-mum		
Sunset Hill J. C. Nichols Inv. Co. Kansas City, Mo.	Building lines on plat	Diff. amts. for diff. types of projections					
Uplands Victoria, B. C.	Main walls 60 ft. from front and side streets	Diff. amts. for diff. types of projections			Prohib-ited	Title re-served by seller	
Uplands Wellesley, Mass.	Main walls 50–25 ft. from front and side streets				Prohib-ited		
Valencia Park Bowie & Trent San Benito, Tex.	On recorded plat						
Vanderlip Sub'n Scarborough, N. Y.	Main walls 40 or 60 ft. from front and side streets				Prohib-ited with-out sell-er's con-sent	Title re-served by seller	
Vinsetta Park Sub'n Vinsetta Land Co. Detroit, Mich.	Set-back 50 ft. from front lot line; 40 ft. also	Projections may violate set-back			Prohib-ited		4 ft. in rear
Wagner-Thoreson Co. Los Angeles, Cal.							
Woodmar Woodmar Realty Co. Hammond, Ind.	Set-back 50 ft. from front line	Projections may enter 50 ft. set-back	60 ft. min-imum				
Westchester William Zelosky Chicago, Ill.	Set-back 15 ft. from front line	Projections may not violate set-back					
Westwood Sub'n Van Alstine Land Co. Detroit, Mich.	Set-back 25 ft. from front and 5 ft. from side lot line	Projections may encroach on set-back					Reserved by seller

on the building line or may the steps encroach on the setback area; if a covered porch must be entirely behind the building line, must an open porch observe the same rule? In other words, a building line must be defined not only in terms of distance from the lot line but also in terms of the portion of the building affected by this line. Still another objection to this type of restrictive clause is that it makes no mention of side lines. No requirements are set with respect to location of the residence in relation to the houses on either side. In short, a building line restriction such as the one cited here is of but little value from the point of view of securing a balanced plan for the development. It marks one extreme in the variety of clauses drawn to establish building lines.

Restrictions in the second classification are much more adequate for the purposes for which they are designed. Two examples in this class may be cited:

"All lots (excepting those fronting on Van Alstine and J. W. Daly Avenues and Maple Avenue west of J. W. Daly Avenue) shall be used for residence purposes only and no building shall be erected or placed within 25 feet from the front lot line, and at least 5 feet from the side lot lines. (Porches, steps and windows, however, shall not be construed as a part of the building)."[17]

"No building shall be erected, placed or suffered to remain on any lot, the front of said building being less than thirty (30) feet from the inside sidewalk line of the street upon which said lot faces, nor shall any building or porch be nearer to the drive side of any lot than eight (8) feet and nearer to the other side than three (3) feet. On lots facing on Avon Center or Armour Roads, however, no building shall be erected, placed or suffered to remain thereon, the front thereof being nearer than forty (40) feet to the inside line of the sidewalk of the street upon which said lot faces, but in all other respects said lots facing on said Roads shall be governed by the same terms and conditions as any and all other Sub Lots in said Subdivision. No open porch shall extend further than ten (10) feet from the building upon any lot."[18]

Other restrictions in this group define somewhat further the building lines for projections. Some clauses stipulate the number of feet which oriels, bays, porches (open or closed), steps, terraces, chimneys, etc., may encroach upon the setback area. In such cases the clause usually reads to the effect that the main walls of the building shall be set back a definite number of feet from the lot line and that projections may protrude a specified number of feet beyond these walls.

The third group of building line restrictions is doubtless possible only on the high-grade subdivisions, for their planning involves considerable expense. To determine them accurately requires a careful survey and a study of the peculiarities of each lot. It is not feasible to reproduce here a restrictive clause of this kind on account of its length and the fact that the data are not readily understandable without reference to a plat of subdivision. Suffice to say, this type of building restriction represents the acme of caution in safeguarding the developer's plan.

Building line regulations also frequently contain requirements as to the location of garages and other outbuildings. Distance from the residence, from the rear line, from the side street are the most common forms of regulation used in these cases.

Closely related to this matter of building lines is regulation of the frontage of residences on particular streets. Such regulation is especially important with reference to corner lots. Carefully drawn instruments, such as those of the

[17] Westwood Subdivision, Van Alstine Land Company, Detroit, Michigan.

[18] Avon Center Estates, H. F. Bowse, Cleveland, Ohio.

J. C. Nichols Investment Company of Kansas City, state which way the residences on separate lots or blocks of lots shall face.

Finally, the easements and rights of way that are reserved are an important restriction on the use of the lot area. A rather common practice with reference to these is merely to refer in the deed to the recorded map on which easements and rights of way are platted, as for instance

"Such easements and rights of way are located on said Map entitled "Fernside" and except where otherwise indicated thereon or specified in conveyances, shall be confined to the rear five feet of all lots shown thereon."[19]

These reservations are usually made only on the rear of the lot, although in some subdivisions both side and rear areas are reserved.

"Rear and side lot lines to the distance of 2 feet, together with overhang for pole arms, are subject to an easement for necessary electric wire or telephone poles or for any utility, and ingress and egress is expressly reserved to workmen employed thereon."[20]

A good deal may be said in favor of considerable elasticity in the administration of building line restrictions. If discretionary powers are vested in the subdivider or his agent, he may make an exception here and there where it seems necessary, securing compensation by a more stringent restriction applied elsewhere on the same lot. Elasticity in administering this restriction should not be exercised to favor a certain lot holder. It is merely a matter of weighing leniency on one point against more strict construction on another in the interest of a better balanced development. When this power is coupled with power to approve building plans, it may result in a more attractive layout than could have been secured by a uniform or definite prescription applied to a larger area.

The only other restriction which has to do with the actual use of the lot area is the one which stipulates the percentage of the lot area that may be covered by the improvement. Certain restrictions state flatly that "no dwelling shall occupy more than 35% of an inside lot or 45% of a corner lot"[21] but a more common form couples percentage of lot area with percentage of lot width to be covered.[22] One of the main benefits of such a restriction is to prevent the erection of various outbuildings on the rear of the lot. It is therefore especially useful when applied to deep lots. The few instances (six) of this type of regulation would seem to indicate that its importance is declining, probably as a result of the growing importance of the restriction requiring approval of building plans and definite stipulations as to the number and kind of outbuildings. The submission of building plans to the subdivider or other agency in charge of administering that restriction affords opportunity for insuring ample free spaces.

Restrictions with respect to the size of the lot in terms of minimum lot frontage or minimum lot area were found in but very few of the deeds examined. The reason is probably that such items are taken care of on the recorded plat of the subdivision. However, a statement as to the minimum lot frontage allowed was found in seven instances in the deeds

---

[19] Fernside, Fred T. Wood Company, Oakland, California.

[20] Maple Hill, Frank B. McKibbin Company, Lansing, Michigan.

[21] Sunrise Addition, R. C. Erskine & Co., Seattle, Wash.

[22] "No residence, with attached garages, attached greenhouses and porches shall occupy to exceed 60% of the area of this lot, nor shall have a width greater than 80% of the width of the lot . . ." (Brown Section, Thorpe Bros., Minneapolis, Minn.).

examined in this study. Its main usefulness would seem to be in preventing the subdivision of original lots into smaller parcels. Whether or not this is the purpose of such clauses is not revealed by the deeds, which contain for the most part flat statements to the effect that "no lot shall have a frontage of less than fifty feet."[23] If the prevention of subdivision is its purpose, this restriction seems rather a left-handed measure of control.

The requirement of a minimum lot area is even more infrequently found, only one subdivision[24] having a stipulation to this effect. The value of this restriction may be impaired unless it is coupled with a requirement for minimum lot frontage. In order to secure the necessary square footage the depth may be extended at the expense of the width. The presence of such a regulation may be explained in some instances by the existence of a state law or a municipal zoning ordinance, which specifies such a minimum.

Much more important are the restrictions aimed directly at further subdivision of the lots. These are more numerous among the examples studied. Many of these clauses merely make a flat statement to the effect that further subdivision of the original lots is prohibited but others include permission to divide the lot and to merge the sections thus created with the adjoining lots, thus

". . . no lot shall be subdivided for the purpose of erecting a complete residence on either portion; provided, however, that a lot may be subdivided when the portions so created are added to the adjoining lots on either side."[25]

The final division under restrictions pertaining to the physical development of the area has to do with regulations regarding the public areas. In general, these restrictions are not very specific. In a large number of the Olmsted deeds a restriction is found which states that the seller reserves title to the public areas but no indication is given as to what these public areas include. Likewise, in the other group of deeds no specific mention is made with reference to public areas, although their existence is evidenced by the presence of maintenance charges which cover the expenses involved in the upkeep of these areas as well as other items which are best handled as community rather than as individual services. One developer specifically reserves riparian rights and another retains title to a piece of marsh land. Whether or not the shores of the lake or the marsh are to be developed for public use is not stated. An occasional developer reserves title to the streets, granting the lot owners easements of ingress and egress over those streets. Such instances are the exception rather than the rule. By far the most common practice is the dedication of the streets to the public. The process is very simple, for if a developer paves his streets, lays sidewalks and sells the adjoining lots without reserving title to the streets, the city regards this as an offer of dedication which it may accept merely by performing such functions as laying sewers or erecting street lights. The whole procedure is frequently regulated by a statute which "usually provides that the recording and acknowledgment of the Subdivision Plat shall operate as a *conveyance in fee simple and with warranty of all streets and alleys* and other portions laid out for public uses."[26] (Italics ours.)

[23] Ashburton Homes, Geo. R. Morris Organization, Baltimore, Md.

[24] Sunrise Addition, R. C. Erskine & Co., Seattle, Wash.

[25] Locust Hills, Blair Homes Co., Altoona, Pa.

[26] MacChesney, *op. cit.*, p. 601–2.

CHAPTER V

Other Clauses Dealing With Duration, Administration, and Racial Restrictions

Restrictions on Alienation and Occupancy

Restrictions regulating ownership and occupancy of subdivision property are usually directed against persons not of the Caucasian race. Thus, when a subdivider inserts a clause in the conveyance to the effect that the lot owner must have the approval of the seller before alienating or renting his property, he is usually seeking to prevent ownership or use of that property by other than white persons. So before discussing in detail what are commonly called "racial restrictions," it may be well to consider briefly the legality of restraints on alienation[1] in general.

The statement has been made that restrictions of a general character against alienation are invalid, whereas a restriction directed against a limited group will generally be sustained.[2] The following quotation expresses a similar idea:

> "A condition may be imposed in a deed on the power of alienation in certain cases, as that the land shall not be conveyed before a certain date or to a certain person . . . But an absolute restriction on the power of alienation . . . is void."[3]

This is not a hard and fast rule, however, for state laws differ and state courts differ in their interpretation of these laws. An Illinois court held that a restriction in a will even for a limited period is invalid,[4] while the United States Supreme Court in the much quoted case of *Cowell* v. *Colorado Springs Co.* upheld the right of an individual to impose such restriction for a limited time. The opinion reads as follows:

> ". . . the owner of property has a right to dispose of it with a limited restriction on its use, however much the restriction may affect the value or the nature of the estate. Repugnant conditions are those which tend to the utter subversion of the estate, such as prohibit entirely the alienation or use of the property. Conditions which prohibit its alienation to particular persons for a limited period, or its subjection to particular uses, are not subversive of the estate: they do not destroy or limit its alienable or inheritable character."[5]

The divergence of opinion which is revealed by these examples is further borne out in the interpretation of restrictions applied to specific racial groups.

In deed restrictions a general restraint upon alienation usually takes the form of a reservation on the part of the seller requiring his approval before the property may be transferred. In the instruments examined only very few instances of this type of restriction were found. Of the 84 deeds but seven contained a clause to this effect and two of these were instruments drawn by the same subdivider. The Shaker Heights development in Cleveland, Ohio, uses this device, although provision is made for overruling the decision of the seller by

[1] Alienation is "the transfer of the property and possession of lands, tenements, or other things, from one person to another." (Bouvier's Law Dictionary, Rawle's Revision, 1914, article on "Alienation".)

[2] See MacChesney, *op. cit.*, p. 586.

[3] Devlin, *op. cit.*, Vol. 2, sec. 965, p. 1791.

[4] "In a devise of land in fee simple a condition against all alienation is void, because repugnant to the estate conveyed . . . A restriction, whether by way of condition or of devise over or against alienation, although for a limited time, of an estate in fee is likewise void, as repugnant to the estate devised to the first taker, by depriving him, during that time, of the inherent power of alienation." *Jones v. Port Huron Engine Co.*, 171 Ill. 502 at 507 (1898).

[5] 100 U. S. 55 at 57 (1879).

the lot owners affected. The warranty deed contains this paragraph:

"The premises hereby conveyed shall not be occupied, leased, rented, conveyed or otherwise alienated, nor shall the title or possession thereof pass to another without the written consent of the Grantor except that the Grantor shall not withhold such consent if and after a written request has been made to the Grantor to permit such occupation, leasing, renting, conveyance or alienation by a majority of the owners of the sublots which adjoin or face said premises upon both sides of the highway or highways, upon which said premises front or abut, and within a distance of five (5) sublots from the respective boundary lines of the said premises, except transfer of title by way of devise or inheritance, in which case the devisee or heir shall take such property subject to the restrictions herein imposed and except that said property may be mortgaged or subjected to judicial sale, provided, in any such case that no purchaser of said premises at judicial sale shall have the right to occupy, lease, rent, convey, or otherwise alienate said premises without the written consent of the Grantor first had and obtained in the manner above stated."

Coming now to racial restrictions, the first question usually asked is: Are they constitutional? The general impression seems to be that an attempt to exclude members of a certain race from a given area is contrary to the law of the land or constitutes racial discrimination. The thirteenth and fourteenth amendments to the Federal Constitution are usually cited in this connection. But these amendments refer to state action or legislative measures and not to individual action based on the right of contract. The principle has therefore been established that legislation cannot segregate racial groups in a community. An outstanding case is that of *Buchanan* v. *Warley*,[6]

[6] "We think this attempt to prevent alienation of the property in question to a person of color was not a legitimate exercise of the police power of the state and is in direct violation of the fundamental law en-

(Continued on page 48)

TABLE III. RESTRICTIONS ON ALIENATION AND OCCUPANCY

Name of Subdivision and Subdivider and Location	Restrictions On Alienation	Restrictions On Occupancy
Alleghany Furnace Baker Estates Altoona, Pa.	Africans, Mongolians prohibited	Africans, Mongolians prohibited
Ardmore J. R. Robertson & Co. Chicago, Ill.	Caucasians only	
Arlington Park Laudermilk Realty Co. Chicago, Ill.		
Armour Hills J. C. Nichols Inv. Co. Kansas City, Mo.	Negroes barred	Negroes barred
Anchorage Heights Anchorage, Ky.		
Ashburton G. R. Morris Org'n Baltimore, Md.	Seller must approve	Seller must approve
Andrews Sub'n New Britain, Conn.		
Avon Center Estates H. F. Bowse Cleveland, Ohio		
Aspinwall Hill Sub'n Brookline, Mass.		
Belmont Country Club A. T. Mc Intosh Co. Chicago, Ill.	Caucasian only—Condition	Caucasian only—Condition
Barton Hills Ann Arbor, Mich.		
Best Manor Fred T. Wood Co. Oakland, Cal.	Caucasians only	Caucasians only
Beacon Falls Beacon Falls, Conn.		
Bonelli-Adams Co. Boston, Mass.		
Bonnycastle Terrace Louisville, Ky.		
Brown Section Thorpe Bros. Minneapolis, Minn.	Caucasians only	Caucasians only
Brookline Hills Sub'n Brookline, Mass.		
Cuyahoga View Heights Hoiles & Hedden Co. Cuyahoga Falls, Ohio	White race only	White race only
Colony Hills Springfield, Mass.		
Cityco Realty Co. Baltimore, Md.	Negroes barred	Negroes barred
Cravath Sub'n Locust Valley, L. I.		
Cushing's Island Casco Bay, Me.		
Deven Heights Hogle & Mawdsley Carmel, Cal.	Asiatics and Negroes barred	Asiatics and Negroes barred
Devonshire Manor Annex Krenn & Dato Chicago, Ill.	Caucasians only—Condition	Caucasians only—Condition

TABLE III. RESTRICTIONS ON ALIENATION AND OCCUPANCY (*Continued*)

Name of Subdivision and Subdivider and Location	Restrictions	
	On Alienation	On Occupancy
Devonshire Manor. Krenn & Dato, Chicago, Ill.	Caucasians only—Condition	Caucasians only—Condition
Diana Gardens. S. S. Berry, Chicago, Ill.		
Estudillo Estates. Fred T. Wood Co., Oakland, Cal.	Caucasians only	Caucasians only
Fairview Addition. Chas. P. Gray Co., Chicago, Ill.		
Fairway Section. Thorpe Bros., Minneapolis, Minn.	Caucasians only	Caucasians only
Forest Hills Gardens. Sage Foundation Homes, Long Island		
Fernside. Fred T. Wood Co., Oakland, Cal.	Africans, Mongolians barred	Caucasians only
Freeman Sub'n. Providence, R. I.		
Gatewood Gardens. R. C. Erskine & Co., Seattle, Wash.	Caucasians only	Caucasians only
Great Neck Hills. Great Neck, L. I.		
Glen Oaks. Guy M. Rush, Los Angeles, Cal.	Caucasians only	Caucasians only
Guilford. Baltimore County, Md.		Negroes barred
Gwin Unit. Fred T. Wood Co., Oakland, Cal.	Caucasians only	Caucasians only
Harroun Park Sub'n. Currier Inv. Co., Detroit, Mich.	Caucasians only	Caucasians only
Highland Park Addition. Krenn & Dato, Inc., Chicago, Ill.	Caucasians only—Condition	Caucasians only—Condition
Howard-Lincoln etc. Add'n. Krenn & Dato, Inc., Chicago, Ill.	Caucasians only—Condition	Caucasians only—Condition
Hunting Ridge. Geo. R. Morris Org'n, Baltimore, Md.	Seller shall approve assignee	Seller shall approve renter
Indian Hill Estates. Bills Realty Co., Chicago, Ill.	Caucasians only	Caucasians only
Kenilworth Hghlds. Sub'n. Wittbold Realty Co., Chicago, Ill.	Caucasians only—Condition	
A. H. Kraus Co. Chicago, Ill.	Caucasians only—Condition	Caucasians only—Condition
Lake Wauconda. Perry Park, Colo.		
Laudermilk Villa. B. H. Laudermilk Co., Chicago, Ill.		

in which the Supreme Court of the United States declared invalid an ordinance of Louisville, Kentucky, designed to prohibit occupancy by a colored person of a house in a block where eight out of ten residences were occupied by white persons.

The right to discriminate through private contract, however, is not so clearly defined, as already indicated. It was hoped that a decisive opinion would be handed down when the Supreme Court considered the case of *Corrigan* v. *Buckley*, which involved the transfer of a piece of property in Washington, D. C., upon which there was a restriction placed by mutual agreement of owners in the block that the several parcels should not be sold to negroes. The court did not give a conclusive decision on this point asserting want of jurisdiction. The opinion in the case, however, may be considered to indicate what the position of the Supreme Court might be when it is called upon to decide such an issue. It suggests an attitude favorable to the free use of the right of contract to control the disposition of property. In fact, so strong is the indication that some proponents of this position are inclined to regard it as authoritative on this point. At any rate the opinion is most interesting and well worth examining. The following excerpts give the gist of the opinion.

"This contention (that the covenant is void in that it is contrary to and forbidden by the 5th, 13th and 14th Amendments) is entirely lacking in substance or color of merit. The fifth Amendment is a limitation only upon the powers of the general government and is not directed against the action of individuals. The thirteenth Amendment involving slavery and involuntary servitude, that is, a condition of enforced compulsory

(*Footnote 6 continued from page 47*)

acted in the 14th amendment of the Constitution preventing state interference with property rights except by due process of law." (245 U. S. 60 (1917).)

service of one to another, does not in other matters protect the individual rights of persons of the negro race. And the prohibitions of the fourteenth Amendment have reference to state action exclusively and not to any action of private individuals. It is state action of a particular character that is prohibited. Individual invasion of individual rights is not the subject matter of the amendment. It is obvious that none of these Amendments prohibited private individuals from entering into contracts respecting the control and disposition of their own property; and there is no color whatever for the contention that they rendered the indenture void."

"Assuming that this contention (that the indenture is void in that it is forbidden by the laws enacted in aid and under the sanction of the thirteenth and fourteenth amendments) drew in question the 'construction' of these statutes, as distinguished from their 'application,' it is obvious upon their face that while they provide inter alia, that all persons and citizens shall have equal right with white citizens to make contracts and acquire property, they, like the constitutional amendments under whose sanction they are enacted, do not in any manner prohibit or invalidate contracts entered into by private individuals in respect to the control and disposition of their own property."[7]

A long line of cases might be cited to show the attitudes of the different state courts. Some of them uphold restraints upon both occupancy and alienation and some uphold them only upon occupancy. An example of the former position is that taken by a Missouri court with reference to a condition in a deed prohibiting for 25 years the sale, lease or rental of the property to a negro.

"It is the rule that an absolute restriction in the power of alienation in the conveyance of a fee simple title is void, but it is entirely within the right and power of the grantor to impose a condition or restraint upon the power of alienation in certain cases to certain persons, or for a certain time, or for certain purposes. The condition in the deed under

[7] 271 U. S. 323; 70 L. ed. 969 at 972 and 973 (1925).

TABLE III. RESTRICTIONS ON ALIENATION AND OCCUPANCY (*Continued*)

Name of Subdivision and Subdivider and Location	Restrictions On Alienation	Restrictions On Occupancy
Lake Shore Highlands, Oakland, Cal.		
Locust Hills, Blair Home Co., Altoona, Pa.	Mongolians and Africans barred	Mongolians and Africans barred
Licton Springs Pk., Seattle, Wash.		
Maple Hill, F. B. McKibbin Co., Lansing, Mich.	Caucasians only	
Manito Park, Spokane, Wash.		
Justin Matthews Co., Little Rock, Ark.		
Milwaukee-Howard etc. Sub'n, Krenn & Dato, Inc., Chicago, Ill.	Caucasians only—Condition	Caucasians only—Condition
Mountain Lake, Lake Wales, Fla.		
Morningside Heights, R. C. Erskine & Co., Seattle, Wash.		
Newton Blvd. Sub'n, Newton, Mass.		
Oak Hill Village, Arnold Hartman, Boston, Mass.		
Oyster Harbor, Inc., F. W. Norris Co., Boston, Mass.		
Pacific Southwest Bank, Los Angeles, Cal.	Caucasians only	Caucasians only
Palos Verdes Estates, Los Angeles, Cal.	Caucasians only	Caucasians only
Redmont Park, Jemison & Co., Birmingham, Ala.		Whites only
Roland Park, Baltimore County, Md.		
St. Francis Wood, Mason-McDuffie Co., San Francisco, Cal.	Caucasians only	Caucasians only
Sackett Sub'n, Louisville, Ky.		
Scarsdale Estates, New York City		
Sudbrook, Baltimore County, Md.		
Shaker Heights, Van Sweringen Co., Cleveland, Ohio		
Sunalta, Calgary, Alberta		
S. Bloomfield Highlands, Michigan Inv. Co., Detroit, Mich.	Caucasians only	Caucasians only
Sunrise Addition, R. C. Erskine & Co., Seattle, Wash.	Caucasians only	Caucasians only

consideration does not come within the rule prohibiting restraints upon alienation."[8]

The California and Michigan courts, however, consider private restrictions on alienation invalid but uphold them when applied to occupancy. An important California case[9] to this effect has already been cited in another connection (Ch. III, p. 16). Two Michigan cases, *Porter* v. *Barrett* and *Parmalee* v. *Morris*,[10] uphold restraints upon occupancy and the former case includes a ruling to the effect that restraints upon alienation are invalid. The problem involved in these cases is not new but the recency of the dates shows that it has been occupying the attention of the courts to a greater extent in the last few years which have witnessed the modern subdivision developments.

This fact is further emphasized by an examination of the deeds included in this study. Forty of the total 84 deeds contain racial restrictions. Of these 33 are restraints both upon alienation and occupancy; four are upon alienation alone; and three upon occupancy only. But more interesting than the numbers in these classes are the sources of the restrictions. Only two of the Olmsted or older group of deeds contain any racial restrictions whatsoever and these are upon occupancy. In other words, 38 of the 40 racial restrictions are found in the more recent instruments.

Any discussion of the geographical distribution of racial restrictions is hampered by the smallness of the sample. Certain tendencies may be noted, however. The device seems to be in rather general use in the vicinity of the larger eastern and northern cities which have experienced a large influx of colored people in recent years. But the most pronounced tendency is found on the Pacific Coast where the restriction is directed primarily against the Orientals. In this connection it is interesting to note that several of the racial restrictions included in the sample cover both alienation and occupancy, in spite of the decision cited previously which shows that restrictions against alienation are not valid under the California Code. The presence of such restrictions merely emphasizes the fact that prohibitions which are technically illegal may continue to exist because they have the

TABLE III. RESTRICTIONS ON ALIENATION AND OCCUPANCY (*Continued*)

Name of Subdivision and Subdivider and Location	Restrictions	
	On Alienation	On Occupancy
Sunnymede Whitcomb & Keller S. Bend, Ind.	Caucasians only, except business	Caucasians only, except business
Sunnyside City Housing Corp. New York City		
Tavern Acres N. Andover, Mass.		
Tilden Realty Corp. Utica, N. Y.		
Sunset Hill J. C. Nichols Inv. Co. Kansas City, Mo.	Negroes barred	Negroes barred
Uplands Victoria, B. C.		
Uplands Wellesley, Mass.		
Valencia Park Bowie & Trent San Benito, Tex.	Caucasians only	Caucasians only
Vanderlip Sub'n Scarborough, N. Y.		
Vinsetta Park Sub'n Vinsetta Land Co. Detroit, Mich.		
Wagner-Thoreson Co. Los Angeles, Cal.	Caucasians only	Caucasians only
Woodmar Woodmar Realty Co. Hammond, Ind.	Caucasians only	Caucasians only
Westchester William Zelosky Chicago, Ill.		
Westwood Sub'n Van Alstine Land Co. Detroit, Mich.	Negroes barred	

[8] *Koehler v. Rowland*, 275 Mo. 573, at 584 (1918).

[9] *Los Angeles Investment Co. v. Gary*, 181 Cal. 680, 186 Pac. 596 (1919); see also *Janss Investment Co. v. Walden*, 196 Cal. 753, 239 Pac. 34 (1925).

[10] 233 Mich. 373 (1925); 218 Mich. 624 (1922).

sanction of the parties to the agreement. As control devices, however, they are precarious because they may be attacked at any time by someone out of sympathy with their purpose and thus easily overthrown.

Of the two forms in which this restriction may be couched, the restrictive covenant is more common than the condition. A typical covenant reads as follows:

"No lot shall be sold, conveyed, leased or rented to any person other than of the white or Caucasian race, nor shall any lot ever be used or occupied by any person other than one of the white or Caucasian race, except such as may be serving as domestics for the owner or tenant of said lot, while said owner or tenant is residing thereon."[11]

An example of a racial restriction in the form of a condition is the one used by Krenn and Dato, of Chicago:

"It shall be an express condition in said Deed that the premises herein described shall not be conveyed or leased by the grantee or any of the successors in title of the grantee to any person who is not a Caucasian; that neither the premises herein described nor any of the improvements thereon shall be occupied by anyone who is not a Caucasian; and that in the event that the premises herein described shall be conveyed or leased by the grantee or any of the successors in title of the grantee to any person who is not a Caucasian, or in the event that said premises or any improvements erected thereon shall at any time be occupied by a person who is not a Caucasian, the property herein described shall revert to the grantor in said deed free and clear from any claim of the grantee or the successor in title of the grantee, such reversion, however, to be subject to any then existing encumbrances."[12]

This discussion serves merely to emphasize the lack of uniformity both in the form of racial restrictions and in the attitude of the courts with respect to them. It therefore behooves each in-

[11] Fairway Section, Thorpe Bros., Minneapolis, Minn.
[12] Highland Park Addition.

TABLE IV. RESTRICTIONS PERTAINING TO THE RIGHTS, POWERS AND DUTIES OF THE SUBDIVIDER

Name of Subdivision and Subdivider and Location	Utility Installation	Reservations and Modifications
Alleghany Furnace......... Baker Estates Altoona, Pa.	Easements reserved by seller	Seller may modify R's on lot use with consent
Ardmore.................. J. R. Robertson & Co. Chicago, Ill.		
Arlington Park............ Laudermilk Realty Co. Chicago, Ill.		
Armour Hills.............. J. C. Nichols Inv. Co. Kansas City, Mo.		Seller may change bldg. lines, frontage, etc.; may assign powers
Anchorage Heights......... Anchorage, Ky.		
Ashburton................. G. R. Morris Org'n Baltimore, Md.		Seller sets bldg. line, grade, etc., in approving plans
Andrews Sub'n............. New Britain, Conn.		
Avon Center Estates....... H. F. Bowse Cleveland, Ohio	Seller reserves right to grant consent for utilities	
Aspinwall Hill Sub'n........ Brookline, Mass.		
Belmont Country Club...... A. T. McIntosh Co. Chicago, Ill.		
Barton Hills............... Ann Arbor, Mich.	Easements reserved by seller	Seller reserves right to modify
Best Manor................ Fred T. Wood Co. Oakland, Cal.		
Beacon Falls............... Beacon Falls, Conn.		
Bonelli-Adams Co.......... Boston, Mass.		
Bonnycastle Terrace........ Louisville, Ky.		
Brown Section............. Thorpe Bros. Minneapolis, Minn.		Seller reserves right to change restrictions with exceptions
Brookline Hills Sub'n....... Brookline, Mass		
Cuyahoga View Heights..... Hoiles & Hedden Co. Cuyahoga Falls, Ohio	Easements reserved by seller	Seller reserves right to modify
Colony Hills............... Springfield, Mass.		
Cityco Realty Co........... Baltimore, Md.		
Cravath Sub'n............. Locust Valley, L. I.	Easements reserved by seller	...

TABLE IV. RESTRICTIONS PERTAINING TO THE RIGHTS, POWERS AND DUTIES OF THE SUBDIVIDER (*Continued*)

Name of Subdivision and Subdivider and Location	Utility Installation	Reservations and Modifications
Cushing's Island .... Casco Bay, Me.		
Deven Heights .... Hogle & Mawdsley Carmel, Cal.		
Devonshire Manor Annex... Krenn & Dato, Inc. Chicago, Ill.	Seller reserves right to petition	
Devonshire Manor......... Krenn & Dato, Inc. Chicago, Ill.	Seller reserves right to petition	
Diana Gardens............ S. S. Berry Chicago, Ill.		
Estudillo Estates.......... Fred T. Wood Co. Oakland, Cal.		
Fairview Addition.......... Chas. P. Gray Co. Chicago, Ill.		
Fairway Section........... Thorpe Brothers Minneapolis, Minn.	Seller reserves right to enter for installation	Seller may modify restrictions with exceptions
Forest Hills Gardens....... Sage Foundation Homes Long Island	Seller reserves right to enter easements	Seller may modify with consent of owners
Fernside................. Fred T. Wood Co. Oakland, Cal.		Modification requires consent of Owners' Assn.
Freeman Sub'n........... Providence, R. I.		
Gatewood Gardens......... R. C. Erskine & Co. Seattle, Wash.		
Great Neck Hills.......... Great Neck, R. I.	Easements reserved by seller	
Glen Oaks................ Guy M. Rush Los Angeles, Cal.		Seller may assign powers; may modify with consent of Assn.
Guilford.................. Baltimore County, Md.		Seller may assign powers; may modify with consent of owners
Gwin Unit................ Fred T. Wood Co. Oakland, Cal.		
Harroun Park Sub'n........ Currier Inv. Co. Detroit, Mich.		
Highland Park Addition.... Krenn & Dato, Inc. Chicago, Ill.	Seller reserves right to petition	
Howard-Lincoln, etc., Add'n. Krenn & Dato Chicago, Ill.		
Hunting Ridge............ George R. Morris Org'n Baltimore, Md.		

dividual subdivider to examine carefully the laws on this point in the state within which he is operating before framing his racial restrictions.

Rights, Powers and Duties of the Subdivider

This section includes a variety of items, one of the most important of which has to do with the provision of improvements and installation of the utilities. In most of the subdivisions included here at least the first improvements have usually been supplied by the developer. Few of the deeds even mention them. An exception is a deed in which the subdivider states that he will provide such improvements as paving, sidewalks, sewer, water and gas mains and electric light lines running to the curb line of the individual lots.

More usual are the deeds which define the easements to be provided for the private utility connections. In the case of such easements it is customary for the seller to reserve the right of ingress and egress upon these easements for the purpose of installing the utilities. A typical restriction of this kind states that

"Easements and rights of way are hereby expressly reserved by The Baker Estates in, upon and over the rear five (5) feet and three (3) feet on each side of each lot shown on the plot, and also in, upon and over the strips of land indicated as reservations, rights of way, streets, lands and paths for the following purposes:

"For the erection, construction and maintenance of poles, wires and conduits, and the necessary or proper attachments in connection therewith for the transmission of electricity for light and power and for telephone and other purposes:

"For the construction and maintenance of storm-water drains, land drains, public and private sewers, pipe lines for supplying gas and water, and for any other public or quasi-public utility or function conducted, maintained, furnished, or performed by or in any method beneath the surface of the ground.

"The Baker Estates shall have the right to enter and to permit others to enter said reserved strip of land for any of the purposes for which said easements and rights of way are reserved.

"The Baker Estates reserves the right at the time of, or after, grading any streets, or any part thereof, to enter upon any abutting lot and grade the portion of such lot adjacent to such street to a slope of 2 to 1, but The Baker Estates shall not be obliged to do such grading or to maintain the slope."[13]

Restrictions of this class should contain, in addition to the right to pass and repass, the right to erect poles or conduits. Failure to include such provision is often a hindrance to utility companies for without it they may be liable for trespass. Adequate easements for utility installation and maintenance are particularly important on private rights of way, i. e., when streets have not been dedicated to the municipality.

The other most common duty with respect to the utilities is the reservation by the subdivider of the right to petition for their installation. A restriction to this effect may read as follows:

"Said Second Party hereby further appoints Bills Realty, Inc., as agent of said Second Party to petition for the installation of sewer, gas and water mains, street lighting and street paving in connection with said premises by special assessment, or to contract for the installation in the streets of said Indian Hill Estates Subdivision or any sewer, water and gas mains, street lights and ornamental posts therefor, street paving, telephone and electric wiring conduits by private contract, and First Party agrees to pay all the installments of such special assessments or the pro rata proportion of the cost thereof, as hereinabove provided, except for sidewalks, street paving and storm sewers."[14]

[13] Alleghany Furnace, The Baker Estates, Altoona, Pa.

[14] Indian Hill Estates, Bills Realty, Inc., Chicago, Ill.

TABLE IV. RESTRICTIONS PERTAINING TO THE RIGHTS, POWERS AND DUTIES OF THE SUBDIVIDER (*Continued*)

Name of Subdivision and Subdivider and Location	Utility Installation	Reservations and Modifications
Indian Hill Estates, Bills Realty Co., Chicago, Ill.	Seller reserves right to petition	
Kenilworth Highlands Sub'n., Wittbold Realty Co., Chicago, Ill.		
A. H. Kraus Co., Chicago, Ill.		
Lake Wauconda, Perry Park, Colo.		
Laudermilk Villa, B. H. Laudermilk Co., Chicago, Ill.		
Lake Shore Highlands, Oakland, Cal.		Seller reserves right to modify
Locust Hills, Blair Home Co., Altoona, Pa.		
Licton Springs Pk., Seattle, Wash.	Right of way reserved	Seller reserves right to modify
Maple Hill, F. B. McKibbin Co., Lansing, Mich.		
Manito Park, Spokane, Wash.		
Justin Matthews Co., Little Rock, Ark.		
Milwaukee-Howard Sub'n., Krenn & Dato, Inc., Chicago, Ill.		
Mountain Lake, Lake Wales, Fla.		Seller may modify with consent of owners
Morningside Heights, R. C. Erskine & Co., Seattle, Wash.		
Newton Blvd. Sub'n, Newton, Mass.		
Oak Hill Village, Arnold Hartman, Boston, Mass.		Modification requires consent of owners
Oyster Harbor, Inc., F. W. Norris Co., Boston, Mass.		
Pacific Southwest Bank, Los Angeles, Cal.		
Palos Verdes Estates, Los Angeles, Cal.		Modification requires consent of owners
Redmont Park, Jemison & Co., Birmingham, Ala.	Seller reserves right to enter and make improvements	Seller reserves right to modify
Roland Park, Baltimore County, Md.		Seller reserves right to assign
St. Francis Wood, Mason-McDuffie Co., San Francisco, Cal.		Seller may assign; may modify with consent of Homes Assn.

TABLE IV. RESTRICTIONS PERTAINING TO THE RIGHTS, POWERS AND DUTIES OF THE SUBDIVIDER (*Continued*)

Name of Subdivision and Subdivider and Location	Utility Installation	Reservations and Modifications
Sackett Sub'n.............. Louisville, Ky.		
Scarsdale Estates........... New York City		Seller reserves unrestricted areas
Sudbrook................. Baltimore County, Md.		Seller reserves right to assign
Shaker Heights............ Van Sweringen Co. Cleveland, Ohio	Seller reserves right to petition	Seller may modify
Sunalta.................. Calgary, Alberta		
S. Bloomfield Highlands..... Michigan Inv. Co. Detroit, Mich.		Modification requires consent of owners
Sunrise Addition........... R. C. Erskine & Co. Seattle, Wash.		
Sunnymede............... Whitcomb & Keller South Bend, Ind.	Easements reserved by seller	Seller reserves unrestricted areas; may assign; may modify with exceptions
Sunnyside................ City Housing Corp. New York City	Installed largely by seller	
Tavern Acres.............. No. Andover, Mass.	Easements reserved on rear lines	
Tilden Realty Corp......... Utica, N. Y.		
Sunset Hill............... J. C. Nichols Inv. Co. Kansas City, Mo.	Easements granted to city; seller will install	
Uplands.................. Victoria, B. C.	Easements reserved	Seller reserves right to modify and assign
Uplands.................. Wellesley, Mass.	Easements reserved on rear lines	
Valencia Park............. Bowie & Trent San Benito, Tex.	Easements reserved	
Vanderlip Sub'n........... Scarborough, N. Y.		Seller may modify height and set-back rules; may assign powers
Vinsetta Park Sub'n........ Vinsetta Land Co. Detroit, Mich.	Provided by seller	
Wagner-Thoreson Co........ Los Angeles, Cal.		
Woodmar................. Woodmar Realty Co. Hammond, Ind.		
Westchester.............. William Zelosky Chicago, Ill.		
Westwood Sub'n........... Van Alstine Land Co. Detroit, Mich.		

Another very important reservation which subdividers frequently make is the retention of the power to alter or modify the restrictive covenants at will. Sometimes this reservation is stated without qualification as

"The seller . . . reserves the right to change or modify the restrictions on this or any property in Redmont Park."[15]

In general the retention of so large a power by the subdivider may be said to be undesirable. It affords an opportunity to manipulate the affairs of the subdivision in his own interest. But in the hands of a conscientious subdivider, one who retains an interest in the development, it may be a good policy, particularly in an emergency in which prompt action is needed. A restriction of this kind would seem to have very definite effect upon the value of the lots in the subdivision. It would produce a feeling of insecurity as to what might happen next, which would tend to lower the price that could be obtained for the lots.

More usual, however, is a qualified reservation of power. Qualifications may take any one of several forms. The subdivider may reserve the right to modify only certain specific restrictions. When this form is used, it is usually only the restrictions pertaining to the physical development of the lots which may be thus arbitrarily modified. As a corollary of this proposition is the qualification which permits the developer to modify certain restrictions only within definite limits. For instance, he may reduce the setback requirement but not bring it below a specified minimum. Another form of qualification is that which states that all clauses except certain designated ones are subject to this power. The exceptions in this case

[15] Jemison & Co., Inc., Birmingham, Ala.

are usually the racial restrictions and those which enforce the developer's zone plan or prevent the intrusion of nuisances. Finally, this power of the subdivider may be limited by requiring the consent of the lot owner or owners affected. These illustrations merely show that the blanket reservation of power to modify as exemplified in the above quotation (p. 54) is the exception rather than the rule. It is impractical to give examples of all the various forms of modification clauses, but the following example is fairly representative and inclusive.

"Provided that the vendor shall have and does hereby reserve the right in the sale and conveyance of any of said lots, to change, alter or annul any of the provisions in the foregoing paragraphs or in any restrictions added hereto, except those in paragraphs numbered 2 and 8 (providing for residential development of all but certain designated lots and for racial restriction) and it may at any time thereafter, with the consent in writing of the then record owner of any lot or lots, change, alter or annul any such provisions as to such lot or lots, or which may, in such sale and conveyance, be established by it, such change to be effectual without the consent of the owners of any other lot or lots, but no change shall be made at any time in the provisions of paragraphs 2 and 8 nor in the other paragraphs which will permit the erection or maintenance of any residence nearer than 30 feet to the front lot line as above provided, nor nearer than 3 feet to either side line, nor shall the required frontage of land to be used and maintained with any residence be reduced more than 5 feet below the minimum number of feet required for each residence without the written consent of the vendor, or its successors, and the consent of 50% of the owners of the other lots in the same block fronting the same street, and of 50% of the owners of the lots in the opposite block fronting the same street."[16]

Another reservation of this same general nature is that by which the subdivider sets aside certain parcels in the subdivision without restrictions.[17] The existence of such areas which are not subject to the same restraints as the other lots in the development may well cause prospective purchasers some uneasiness. An unwise use of these areas could seriously injure the entire development and uncertainty as to their probable use might retard sales in the subdivision, at least sales of lots contiguous to or within the influence of those unrestricted parcels. From the point of view of both subdivider and lot purchaser the wisdom of this reservation of power may be questioned.

A final consideration in this section is the subdivider's reservation of the right to assign his powers and duties to another. This does not mean that he will sell out his interest to another who would be free to ignore the obligations originally assigned to the developer. The clause conveying the right to assign generally contains the provision that the assignee will undertake the duties of the original subdivider as set forth in the deed. The following paragraph states this position clearly:

"Any or all of the rights and powers of Westgate Park Company herein contained may be assigned to any corporation or association which is now organized or which may hereafter be organized, and which will assume the duties of Westgate Park Company hereunder pertaining to the particular rights and powers assigned, and upon any such corporation or association evidencing its consent in writing to accept such assignment and assume such duties, it shall, to the extent of such assignment, have the same rights and powers and be subject to the same obligations and duties as are given to and assumed by Westgate Park Company herein."[18]

---

[16] Brown Section, Thorpe Bros., Minneapolis, Minn.

[17] ". . . the parcels marked 'Reserved' on said map are not restricted in any way." (Scarsdale Estates, New York City).

[18] St. Francis Wood, Mason-McDuffie Co., San Francisco, Calif.

The clauses which outline the rights, powers and duties of the subdivider are likely to undergo considerable change in the future. With the increase of "subdivision developments," as opposed to mere "subdivisions," these clauses will have to be expanded and refined to cover the added responsibilities which such developments will entail for the subdivider. Elasticity and flexibility in these restrictions are essential to securing a well-balanced development. But it should be emphasized that these discretionary powers vested in the subdivider should be applied strictly as an administrative function, that is, in promoting the developer's plan for the physical development of the area and not as a merchandising function to promote the quick sale of lots.

Duration of Restrictions

Discussion of the duration of deed restrictions falls logically into two parts: (1) consideration of the original term for which such clauses are drawn, and (2) length of the periods as well as the methods provided for continuing these restrictions.

Determination of the original terms of deed restrictions is not so simple as would appear, for many instruments contain a statement, for example, to the effect that "all of the restrictions, conditions, covenants, charges and agreements contained herein shall run with the land and continue until January first, 1950." The date when such clauses originated is not given, hence the difficulty in ascertaining accurately their duration in years. Information as to duration has been secured for 52 of the 84 deeds examined. In the case of the Olmsted group, actual duration was given in 20 of the 29 instances. Of the group of 55 newer instruments, actual duration was given in 18 cases and it was possible to secure a fairly accurate estimate of duration for 14 other subdivisions. In all cases where estimates were made the date of termination was given in the deed. In order to determine the date of origination reference was made to such items as the date on which the plat of subdivision was filed, the date when payments should begin, the date by which certain first improvements would be completed, the date of the form, etc. But throughout the discussion the distinction will be maintained between the durations which are specifically stated and those which have been estimated.

The findings as to durations in the various groups of restrictions may be summarized as follows:

Groups of Restrictions	Number of Cases	Average Duration in Years
Total	52	34.4
Olmsted Group		
Actual duration	20	39.7
New group		
Actual duration	18	27.4
Estimated duration	14	35.9*

* This figure includes the very long period (estimated at 101 years) of the restrictions drawn by the Van Sweringen Co. of Cleveland, O., for Shaker Heights. This period is so exceptionally long that it seemed advisable to calculate the average for this group without this figure. Therefore the average for the remaining 13 restrictions is 30.8 years, which gives a truer picture of the facts for this group and puts it more in line with that portion of the group for which the actual data are available.

A surprising degree of uniformity is revealed by these figures. The durations tend to cluster about the 33-year mark, or the length of a generation which is held by some students of the problem to be a logical term for restrictions. Proponents of 33-year restrictions argue that a man buys a homesite when he is starting his career and under the protection of a 33-year restriction he is able to live most of his life there. By the end of that time his family wants to move away and the restriction will have served its purpose. The findings of this analysis are therefore particularly interesting in the light of this contention. The discussion thus far is not to be interpreted as advocating a 33-year duration for restrictive clauses. The term should be decided in the light of certain economic factors which exist for each particular subdivision. These will be discussed later.

Comparison of the average duration of restrictions for the Olmsted group and for the new group shows 39.7 years for the former and 31.1 years for the latter. This difference may be explained in part by the differences in the properties covered. The Olmsted group probably represents a higher general level of development than does the newer group and it seems to be true in general that the more highly developed the subdivision, the longer the term of the restrictions. For example, the duration in Shaker Heights is 101 years, Roland Park 63 years, Glen Oaks 46 years, etc. Another explanation for the difference may be found in the increased rapidity of city growth which is a particularly dominating influence in the cases included in the newer group. In other words, the speed with which land changes from one use to another as a result of city growth makes the subdivider hesitate to bind the land to a given usage for a very long period.

The difficulties inherent in deciding upon the proper duration of restrictions are numerous. In the first place it is absolutely necessary to set a definite time limit. Otherwise the restrictions would be judged invalid as against public policy under the "rule of perpetuities." The rule against perpetuities is used here in its less technical sense to represent the idea of remoteness.[19] The law does not

[19] *Bouvier*, *op. cit.*, article on "Perpetuity." " 'The original meaning of a perpetuity is an inalienable,

(*Continued on page 58*)

TABLE V. DURATION OF RESTRICTIONS

Name of Subdivision and Subdivider and Location	Original Term	Provisions for Extension
Alleghany Furnace; Baker Estates; Altoona, Pa.	25 yrs.	20 yr. period with consent of owners of ⅔ area.
Ardmore; J. R. Robertson & Co.; Chicago, Ill.		
Arlington Park; Loudermilk Realty Co.; Chicago, Ill.		
Armour Hills; J. C. Nichols Inv. Co.; Kansas City, Mo.	25 yrs.	25 yr. period with consent of owners of 51% front ft.
Anchorage Heights; Anchorage, Ky.	35 yrs.	
Ashburton; G. R. Morris Org'n; Baltimore, Md.		
Andrews Sub'n; New Britain, Conn.	48 yrs.	75% of owners may extend period
Avon Center Estates; H. F. Bowse; Cleveland, Ohio		
Aspinwall Hill Sub'n; Brookline, Mass.		
Belmont Country Club; A. T. McIntosh Co.; Chicago, Ill.		
Barton Hills; Ann Arbor, Mich.	28 yrs.	20 yr. period with consent of owners of ⅔ of land
Best Manor; Fred T. Wood Co.; Oakland, Cal.	To 1950	
Beacon Falls; Beacon Falls, Conn.		
Bonelli-Adams Co.; Boston, Mass.		
Bonnycastle Terrace; Louisville, Ky.	58 yrs.	
Brown Section; Thorpe Bros.; Minneapolis, Minn.	To 1964	
Brookline Hills Sub'n; Brookline, Mass.	36 yrs.	
Cuyahoga View Heights; Hoiles & Hedden Co.; Cuyahoga Falls, Ohio	1976	Continue indefinitely
Colony Hills; Springfield, Mass.	1950	20 yr. period with consent of owners of ⅔ of land
Cityco Realty Co.; Baltimore, Md.		
Cravath Sub'n; Locust Valley, L. I.	1971	By 6 owners of original lots
Cushing's Island; Casco Bay, Me.		
Deven Heights; Hogle & Mawdsley; Carmel, Cal.		
Devonshire Manor Annex; Krenn & Dato, Inc.; Chicago, Ill.	To 1960	

TABLE V. DURATION OF RESTRICTIONS (*Continued*)

Name of Subdivision and Subdivider and Location	Original Term	Provisions for Extension
Devonshire Manor........... Krenn & Dato, Inc. Chicago, Ill.	To 1950	
Diana Gardens............... S. S. Berry Chicago, Ill.		
Estudillo Estates............. Fred T. Wood Co. Oakland, Cal.	To 1950	
Fairview Addition............ Chas. P. Gray Co. Chicago, Ill.	20 yrs.	
Fairway Section............. Thorpe Brothers Minneapolis, Minn.	To 1964	
Forest Hills Gardens.......... Sage Foundation Homes Long Island	To 1950	20 yr. period with consent of owners of ⅗ area
Fernside.................... Fred T. Wood Co. Oakland, Cal.	To 1950	20 yr. period with consent of owners of 65% area
Freeman Sub'n............. Providence, R. I.	To 1955	
Gatewood Gardens........... R. C. Erskine & Co. Seattle, Wash.		
Great Neck Hills............. Great Neck, L. I.	To 1940	
Glen Oaks.................. Guy M. Rush Los Angeles, Cal.	To 1973	20 yr. period with consent of owners of ½ area
Guilford.................... Baltimore County, Md.	To 1950	20 yr. period with consent of ⅗ owners
Gwin Unit.................. Fred T. Wood Co. Oakland, Cal.	To 1950	
Harroun Park Sub'n.......... Currier Inv. Co. Detroit, Mich.		
Highland Park Addition...... Krenn & Dato, Inc. Chicago, Ill.	To 1960	
Howard-Lincoln, etc., Sub'n... Krenn & Dato, Inc. Chicago, Ill.	To 1960	
Hunting Ridge............... Geo. R. Morris Org'n Baltimore, Md.		
Indian Hill Estates........... Bills Realty Co. Chicago, Ill.		
Kenilworth Hglds. Subd'n..... Wittbold Realty Co. Chicago, Ill.		
A. H. Kraus Co.............. Chicago, Ill.		
Lake Wauconda.............. Perry Park, Colo.		
Laudermilk Villa............. B. H. Laudermilk Co. Chicago, Ill.		

favor an interest which vests to a remote period. This attitude is in harmony with the economic point of view which recognizes the undesirability of the present tying the hands of the future. This principle is particularly significant in its application to transactions involving real estate because of the long-time effect of an individual's act when applied to land. In determining the exact period of the restrictions two major elements are to be considered: (1) the character of the proposed development and (2) the character and expected growth of the community of which the subdivision is a part.

There are two aspects to the problem of the relation of the character of the development to the duration of the restrictive covenants. The most important is to make sure that the restrictions shall continue in force long enough to establish the character of the district. In other words, the minimum duration must cover the period of sale and the period required to see the major portion of the area built up. Some hold that this minimum duration is sufficient, arguing that the built-up area can maintain itself sufficiently against encroaching uses. Others, however, favor a longer restrictive period on the ground that the development should be protected during its probable life in the use for which it was originally designed. The latter position appears to be more logical, for it would seem that protection is most desirable when the investment is complete. The intrusion of an inharmonious use into a built-up area would seem to be

(*Footnote 19 continued from page 57*)
indestructible interest. The second artificial meaning is an interest which will not vest to a remote period. This latter is the meaning which is attached to the term when the rule against perpetuities is spoken of;' (Gray, Perp. §140.) The author last cited considers it a matter of regret that the rule should not have been known as the rule against remoteness, rather than the rule as against perpetuities."

more serious than such intrusion into a comparatively unbuilt district.

The second aspect has to do with the kind of development which it is proposed to create. It is impractical to put a 30- or 40-year term on restrictions in connection with a development for medium-priced homes. The improvements on such subdivisions cannot be expected to have as long a life as those in the high-priced developments. The rate of obsolescence is more rapid. Thus, the house may have deteriorated seriously in 25 years. But rather than spend a considerable amount on it the owner will let it continue to run down for the balance of the restriction period, particularly if the type of use is likely to change at the end of the period. A relation should therefore be established between the life of the improvement and the duration of the restriction.

A more important factor in the determination of proper duration is the expected growth of the city. In a city which is growing rapidly it is obviously wise to restrict property for a shorter period than in a city of slower growth. Two results of failure to calculate duration properly may be noted. From the point of view of the city unwise restrictions may create blighted districts which stand in the way of the natural growth of the city. From the point of view of the owners of the restricted property, they may no longer supply the protection which was their aim. If the city grows up around them and different uses come up to the very borders of the subdivision, the character of the community may be practically ruined. This process may be called the obsolescence of restrictions.

Extension of Restrictions

The extension of the period of restriction consists of three elements: (1) the

TABLE V. DURATION OF RESTRICTIONS
(*Continued*)

Name of Subdivision and Subdivider and Location	Original Term	Provisions for Extension
Lake Shore Highlands........ Oakland, Cal.	To 1950	20 yr. period with consent 65% of land
Locust Hills.................. Blair Home Co. Altoona, Pa.	20 yrs.	20 yr. period
Licton Springs Pk............ Seattle, Wash.	To 1965	
Maple Hill.................. F. B. McKibbin Co. Lansing, Mich.		
Manito Park................ Spokane, Wash.		
Justin Matthews Co.......... Little Rock, Ark.		
Milwaukee-Howard Sub'n...... Krenn & Dato, Inc. Chicago, Ill.	To 1960	
Mountain Lake............... Lake Wales, Fla.	To 1940	20 yr. period with consent of majority
Morningside Heights......... R. C. Erskine & Co. Seattle, Wash.	To 1930	
Newton Blvd. Sub'n.......... Newton, Mass.	To 1930	
Oak Hill Village............. Arnold Hartman Boston, Mass.	30 yrs.	
Oyster Harbor, Inc.......... F. W. Norris Co. Boston, Mass.		
Pacific Southwest Bank....... Los Angeles, Cal.	To 1936	
Palos Verdes Estates......... Los Angeles, Cal.	37 yrs.	20 yr. period with consent of owners of ½ area
Redmont Park............... Jemison & Co. Birmingham, Ala.		
Roland Park................ Baltimore County, Md.	To 1960	
St. Francis Wood............ Mason-McDuffie Co. San Francisco, Cal.	33 yrs.	20 yr. period with consent of owners of ½ area
Sackett Sub'n................ Louisville, Ky.		
Scarsdale Estates............ New York City		
Sudbrook................... Baltimore County, Md.	To 1920	
Shaker Heights.............. Van Sweringen Co. Cleveland, Ohio	To 2026	Continuous; changed by consent of owners in block
Sunalta..................... Calgary, Alberta		
S. Bloomfield Highlands....... Michigan Inv. Co. Detroit, Mich.	To 1945	

TABLE V. DURATION OF RESTRICTIONS
(*Continued*)

Name of Subdivision and Subdivider and Location	Original Term	Provisions for Extension
Sunrise Addition R. C. Erskine & Co. Seattle, Wash.		
Sunnymede Whitcomb & Keller South Bend, Ind.	25 yrs.	10 yr. period with consent of owners of 51% front ft.
Sunnyside City Housing Corp. New York City		
Tavern Acres No. Andover, Mass.	To 1970	
Tilden Realty Corp. Utica, N. Y.		
Sunset Hill J. C. Nichols Inv. Co. Kansas City, Mo.	25 yrs.	25 yr. period with consent of owners of 51% front ft.
Uplands Victoria, B. C.	To 1965	
Uplands Wellesley, Mass.	To 1970	
Valencia Park Bowie & Trent San Benito, Tex.	15 yrs.	
Vanderlip Sub'n Scarborough, N. Y.	To 1945	With consent of 75% of owners
Vinsetta Park Sub'n Vinsetta Land Co. Detroit, Mich.	To 1935	20 yr. period with consent of owners of ⅔ area
Wagner-Thoreson Co. Los Angeles, Cal.		
Woodmar Woodmar Realty Co. Hammond, Ind.	50 yrs.	After 20 yrs. 60% frontage may ask abrogation
Westchester William Zelosky Chicago, Ill.	To 1970	
Westwood Sub'n Van Alstine Land Co. Detroit, Mich.	To 1935	20 yrs. with consent of owners of ⅔ lots

length of the extension period; (2) the legal procedure involved in the extension; and (3) the question of who has the power to make such extension. The most common length of the extension period is 20 years, with an occasional 10- or 25-year period mentioned. The legal procedure usually involves the execution of a formal statement which sets forth the intention to continue the restrictions and which shall be filed with the recorder of deeds within a specified time before the expiration of the original term.

Somewhat less uniform are the provisions with respect to the consent of the owners required for such a continuation. The necessary number is defined in various ways: the owners of a certain percentage of the front footage in the subdivision, the owners of a certain percentage of the total area, or a certain percentage of all the owners.

A typical restriction embodying these points follows:

"At the end of this time, January 1, 1950, the above restrictions shall be extended for a period of twenty years from that date and thereafter for successive periods of twenty (20) years. On the date of expiration of each extension the restrictions may be removed, modified or altered for the whole or part of the restricted area, if one year prior to January 1, 1950, and one year prior to the expiration of each extension, appropriate instruments in writing, consenting to the removal, modification or alteration of the restrictions, shall be signed, executed and acknowledged by the owners (including The Baker Estates, if they still retain the fee to one or more lots, but not including mortgagees) of not less than two-thirds of the land included in said tract, exclusive of streets and parks intended for the general use of the owners of the land included in said tract; and provided, further, that any such removal may be made for the whole or part of above mentioned area, with the provision that in no case the area shall be less than the total frontage within a block on a certain street or avenue, and provided further, that such instrument shall be filed with the Recorder of Deeds of Blair County at least one year prior to the expiration of the first twenty-five (25) year period or any of the twenty (20) year periods afterward."[20]

A restriction of this nature places the burden upon those lot owners who wish to alter the restrictions. In other words, the restriction provides for the automatic renewal of the covenants for 20-year periods unless provision for modification is made according to certain prescribed rules. But those lot owners who are desirous of making alterations are charged with the responsibility of

[20] Alleghany Furnace, Baker Estates, Altoona, Pa.

initiating them. This method is most common and is advocated by such a well known developer as Mr. J. C. Nichols. Others, including Mr. Bouton, the developer of Roland Park, advocate placing the burden on those who wish to extend the restrictions.

An interesting proposal in connection with the whole problem of the duration of restrictive argeements is that provision be made for the breaking of such restrictions upon consent of a majority of the owners. One objection to this proposal is that 51% is a rather small margin. Besides, although a majority of the owners may be ready to transfer their property to a higher use, the city or surrounding area may not be able to absorb at once or even within a reasonable time the total area of the subdivision which would be thrown open to the higher use by the vote of 51% of the lot owners. Furthermore, only a small part of the lot owners will be able to take advantage of the higher use and the others not so favorably situated will suffer as a result.

In summarizing it should be emphasized that no general rule can be laid down for determining the proper duration of deed restrictions. This matter must be calculated for each individual subdivision in the light of the conditions which will influence its future. There are certain limits, however, within which this determination of proper duration will take place. The minimum length of the restrictions will be such as to insure approximately complete development of the tract. The subdivider must protect the area until its character is established. At the same time he does not want to preclude the transition of that property into a higher use when that use is economically advisable. Therefore, the maximum limit of the duration will be determined by the expectancy of change in use. But the

TABLE VI. CLAUSES PROVIDING FOR ENFORCEMENT OF RESTRICTIONS

Name of Subdivision and Subdivider and Location	By Whom	What Means
Alleghany Furnace..... Baker Estates Altoona, Pa.	Run with land	Remove or abate violation
Ardmore.............. J. R. Robertson & Co. Chicago, Ill.		
Arlington Park......... Laudermilk Realty Co. Chicago, Ill.		
Armour Hills.......... J. C. Nichols Inv. Co.. Kansas City, Mo.	Run with land.	Injunction to prevent violation
Anchorage Heights..... Anchorage, Ky.		
Ashburton............. G. R. Morris Org'n Baltimore, Md.		
Andrews Sub'n......... New Britain, Conn.	Reserved by seller	
Avon Center Estates ... H. F. Bowse Cleveland, Ohio	Run with land	Entering to abate or by bill of equity
Aspinwall Hill Sub'n.... Brookline, Mass.		
Belmont Country Club . A. T. McIntosh Co. Chicago, Ill.	Run with land	
Barton Hills........... Ann Arbor, Mich.		Abate at owner's expense
Best Manor........... Fred T. Wood Co. Oakland, Cal.		Reversion to seller on violation
Beacon Falls........... Beacon Falls, Conn.		
Bonelli-Adams Co...... Boston, Mass.		
Bonnycastle Terrace.... Louisville, Ky.		Enter to abate at owner's expense
Brown Section......... Thorpe Bros. Minneapolis, Minn.	Owners' Ass'n	
Brookline Hills Sub'n... Brookline, Mass.		Entrance to abate or by law
Cuyahoga View Heights. Hoiles & Hedden Co. Cuyahoga Falls, Ohio	Run with land	Seller may enter and abate at expense of owner
Colony Hills........... Springfield, Mass.		Abate at owner's expense
Cityco Realty Co....... Baltimore, Md.	Run with land	
Cravath Sub'n......... Locust Valley, L. I.		By courts
Cushing's Island....... Casco Bay, Me.		
Deven Heights......... Hogel & Mawdsley Carmel, Cal.	Run with land	
Devonshire Manor Annex Krenn & Dato, Inc. Chicago, Ill.	Seller and owners	

TABLE VI. CLAUSES PROVIDING FOR ENFORCEMENT OF RESTRICTIONS
(*Continued*)

Name of Subdivision and Subdivider and Location	By Whom	What Means
Devonshire Manor..... Krenn & Dato, Inc. Chicago, Ill.		
Diana Gardens......... S. S. Berry Chicago, Ill.		
Estudillo Estates....... Fred T. Wood Co. Oakland, Cal.		Reversion to seller
Fairview Addition...... Chas. P. Gray Co. Chicago, Ill.	Run with land	
Fairway Section....... Thorpe Brothers Minneapolis, Minn.		
Forest Hills Gardens.... Sage Found'n Homes Long Island	Seller and owners	Seller may enter to abate
Fernside.............. Fred T. Wood Co. Oakland, Cal.	Run with land	Seller and owners' assn. may enter and abate
Freeman Sub'n........ Providence, R. I.		
Gatewood Gardens..... R. C. Erskine & Co. Seattle, Wash.	Run with land	
Great Neck Hills....... Great Neck, L. I.		
Glen Oaks............. Guy M. Rush Los Angeles, Cal.	Homes Assn. Run with land	Reversion to seller or Assn. may abate
Guilford.............. Baltimore Co., Md.		Enter and abate
Gwin Unit............ Fred T. Wood Co. Oakland, Cal.	Run with land	Reversion to seller
Harroun Park Sub'n.... Currier Inv. Co. Detroit, Mich.		
Highland Park Add'n... Krenn & Dato, Inc. Chicago, Ill.		
Howard-Lincoln, etc. Add'n.............. Krenn & Dato, Inc. Chicago, Ill.	Sellers and owners	
Hunting Ridge......... Geo. R. Morris Org'n. Baltimore, Md.		
Indian Hill Estates..... Bills Realty Co. Chicago, Ill.		
Kenilworth Highlands Sub'n.............. Wittbold Realty Co. Chicago, Ill.		
A. H. Kraus Co........ Chicago, Ill.	Run with land	
Lake Wauconda........ Perry Park, Colo.		
Laudermilk Villa....... B. H. Laudermilk Co. Chicago, Ill.		

determination of both of these limits constitutes a problem in forecasting and is subject to all the difficulties inherent in that process.

A question might be raised as to whether modifications of restrictions would constitute valid grounds for not enforcing the remaining clauses. The consensus of opinion seems to be that, if the alteration did not impair the benefit of the scheme, the balance of the restrictions would continue to be enforceable.[21] The concept of privity estate is the foundation upon which such opinion rests. It also illustrates the importance which the courts attach to a general plan for improvement of the area.

Enforcement of Restrictions

This section divides itself logically into two parts: (1) the agencies by which the restrictions may be enforced and (2) the powers that may be employed in the enforcing process.

First of all, the subdivider may reserve to himself the right to enforce the restrictions, but this reservation is uncommon. The disadvantage of such a provision is patent. The subdivider's interest ceases with the selling out of the subdivision and his departure removes the enforcing agent. The usual practice is to designate these restrictive agreements as covenants running with the land, thus making them enforceable by owners of the benefited land. A typical example of this type of provision reads as follows:

"The herein enumerated restrictions, reservations, agreements and covenants shall be deemed as covenants and not as conditions hereof and shall run with the land and shall bind the Grantee, heirs, executors, administrators and assigns . . . and the provisions herein contained shall bind and inure to the benefit of and be enforceable by the

[21] *Sanford v. Keer*, 80 N. J. Eq. 240, 83 Atl. 225 (1912).

Grantor and by the owner or owners, of any property in said Allotment, their legal representatives, heirs, executors and assigns, and failure of the Grantor or any property owner to enforce any of such restrictions, covenants provisions and agreements herein contained shall in no event be deemed a waiver of the right to do so thereafter."[22]

Another agency of enforcement which is becoming increasingly important is the owners' association. The efficiency of such an organization as an enforcing agent depends, of course, upon the organization itself, i.e., whether it is an active or only a perfunctory body, whether it is legally constituted or an informal association. This question of organization and powers will be discussed in a subsequent section. If it operates efficiently and thoroughly, it no doubt makes an excellent enforcing medium, for it represents the interests of the entire area and from the owners' point of view.

The statement has been made that restrictive covenants should be enforceable by the city.[23] The answer to the question of who may enforce restrictions lies in the answer to the question of who is the owner of the land benefited thereby. As a matter of law, only the owners of the benefited land have the powers of enforcing covenants. Certain restrictions, such as setbacks, might well be considered to be drawn for the benefit of the city. In fact, instances of this exist. Mr. Robert Whitten in response to further questioning about enforcement by a municipality cited instances in which "the Cleveland Planning Commission has in practice . . . required subdividers of residence property to place a building line on the subdivision plat and

[22] Cuyahoga View Heights, Hoiles and Hedden, Cuyahoga Falls, Ohio.

[23] See Robert Whitten, *A Research into the Economics of Land Subdivisions* (Syracuse: School of Citizenship and Public Affairs of Syracuse University and Regional Plan of New York and its Environs, 1927) p. 12.

TABLE VI. CLAUSES PROVIDING FOR ENFORCEMENT OF RESTRICTIONS (*Continued*)

Name of Subdivision and Subdivider and Location	By Whom	What Means
Lake Shore Highlands . . Oakland, Cal.	Right reserved by seller	
Locust Hills. . . . . Blair Home Co. Altoona, Pa.	Run with land	Seller may enter and abate
Licton Springs Pk. . . . . . Seattle, Wash.		Seller may enter and abate
Maple Hill. . . . . F. B. McKibbin Co. Lansing, Mich.	Run with land	
Manito Park. . . . . Spokane, Wash.		
Justin Matthews Co. . . . Little Rock, Ark.		
Milwaukee-Howard, etc. Sub'n. . . . . Krenn & Dato, Inc. Chicago, Ill.	Run with land	
Mountain Lake. . . . . Lake Wales, Fla.		Enter and abate
Morningside Heights . . . R. C. Erskine & Co. Seattle, Wash.		
Newton Blvd. Sub'n. . . . Newton, Mass.		
Oak Hill Village. . . . . Arnold Hartman Boston, Mass.		Remedies at law. Enter and abate
Oyster Harbor, Inc. . . . . F. W. Norris Co. Boston, Mass.	Seller and owners	
Pacific Southwest Bank. Los Angeles, Cal.		Reversion. Entry to abate
Palos Verdes Estates . . . Los Angeles, Cal.	Seller and owners	Reversion to seller
Redmont Park. . . . . Jemison & Co. Birmingham, Ala.		
Roland Park. . . . . Baltimore Co., Md.	Seller	
St. Francis Wood. . . . . . . Mason-McDuffie Co. San Francisco, Cal.	Run with land	Seller may enter and abate
Sackett Sub'n. . . . . Louisville, Ky.		
Scarsdale Estates. . . . . . . New York City		
Sudbrook. . . . . Baltimore Co., Md.		$10 fine per day after notice to correct
Shaker Heights. . . . . Van Sweringen Co. Cleveland, Ohio	Run with land	Seller may enter and abate; reentry for breach of condition
Sunalta. . . . . Calgary, Alberta		
S. Bloomfield Hghlds. . . Michigan Inv. Co. Detroit, Mich.	Run with land	

TABLE VI. CLAUSES PROVIDING FOR ENFORCEMENT OF RESTRICTIONS
(*Continued*)

Name of Subdivision and Subdivider and Location	By Whom	What Means
Sunrise Addition, R. C. Erskine & Co., Seattle, Wash.	Run with land	-
Sunnymede, Whitcomb & Keller, South Bend, Ind.	Run with land	
Sunnyside, City Housing Corp., New York City		
Tavern Acres, No. Andover, Mass.	Owners	
Tilden Realty Corp., Utica, N. Y.		
Sunset Hill, J. C. Nichols Inv. Co., Kansas City, Mo.	Run with land	
Uplands, Victoria, B. C.		Enter and abate at owner's expense
Uplands, Wellesley, Mass.	Owners	
Valencia Park, Bowie & Trent, San Benito, Tex.	Run with land	Reversion
Vanderlip Sub'n, Scarborough, N. Y.		
Vinsetta Park Sub'n, Vinsetta Land Co., Detroit, Mich.	Run with land	
Wagner-Thoreson Co., Los Angeles, Cal.	Run with land	Reversion in some cases; also re-entry
Woodmar, Woodmar Realty Co., Hammond, Ind.	Owners	
Westchester, William Zelosky, Chicago, Ill.	Run with land	Reversion
Westwood Sub'n, Van Alstine Land Co., Detroit, Mich.	Run with land	

to state on the plat that the building lines were established for the benefit of the city as well as for the benefit of the individual lot owners and that they were enforceable by the city as well as by the lot owners." These acts were "without any legal authority" and it is doubtful whether they would be upheld at law. Even though in the evolution of legal opinion courts should eventually sanction such practice in these instances, the same principle would not be applicable to other restrictions such as those specifying single-family residences or all drives to be on the left side of the house. It is a fact, however, that municipalities do benefit from private restrictions through economies in improvement at least, even though they may not enforce these clauses.

With respect to enforcement two methods are employed depending on whether the restriction is a covenant or a condition. As the reader will recall, in the case of covenants of the type discussed here the usual remedy is found in equity in the form of an injunction to restrain the violation. This is the accepted procedure. Yet even in the restrictive agreements of some of the best subdivisions it is not uncommon to find an attempt on the part of the subdivider to go further in enforcing the restrictions. Frequently, under a clause headed "right to abate," he asserts a right to enter the premises and abate the violation.

"Violation of any restriction or condition or breach of any covenant or agreement herein contained shall give The Baker Estates, in addition to all other remedies, the right to enter upon the land upon or as to which such violation or breach consists, and summarily to abate and remove, at the expense of the owner thereof, any erection, thing or condition that may exist thereon contrary to the intent and meaning of the provisions hereof; and The Baker Estates shall not thereby be deemed guilty of any manner of trespass for such entry, abatement or removal, nor be liable to any damages occasioned thereby."[24]

An attempt to act on the strength of such a provision, however, seems dangerous, for the enforcing agent would probably be liable for trespass. It may be useful as a basis for procedure after injunctive relief has been granted by the court. In the main, however, a clause of this sort appears rather as a gesture on

[24] Alleghany Furnace, Baker Estates, Altoona, Pa.

the part of the subdivider than as a workable restriction. The matter of construing covenants and conditions was discussed in Chapter III. It is sufficient, therefore, at this point merely to reiterate that attempts to enforce restrictions by a reverter clause are likely to fail because the courts do not favor insecure titles which are involved in "conditions subsequent."

However, certain circumstances justify the use of a condition and if the intention of the parties is clear the courts will sustain the restriction. It therefore behooves the subdivider to be cautious in the use of the reverter clause for such a clause gains weight from limited and well-considered use. In other words, a particularly important restriction, such as the prohibition of ownership and occupancy by non-Caucasians, may well be designated as a condition subsequent; thus

> "It shall be an express condition in said deed that the premises herein described shall not be conveyed or leased by the grantee or any of the successors in title of the grantee, to any person who is not a Caucasian; that neither the premises herein described nor any of the improvements thereon shall be occupied by anyone who is not a Caucasian; and that in the event that the premises herein described shall be conveyed or leased by the grantee or any of the successors in title of the grantee to any person who is not a Caucasian, or in the event that said premises or any improvements erected thereon shall at any time be occupied by a person who is not a Caucasian, the property herein described shall revert to the grantor in said deed free and clear from any claim of the grantee or the successors in title of the grantee, such reversion, however, to be subject to any then existing encumbrance."[25]

In addition to the critical attitude of the courts, an economic question may be raised with respect to the use of conditions. One of the subdivider's chief aims is to dispose of his interest in the property as quickly as possible. He is usually very definite in his unwillingness to resell properties for his original purchasers. Therefore, it seems unlikely except in very urgent cases that he would be anxious to enforce a restriction which would bring the property back into his hands for resale. Furthermore, when the enforcing agent is an owners' association, problems may easily arise. For instance, how could such an organization be constituted legally to enable it to receive title to a piece of property as a result of the operation of a reverter clause, for "reversion" implies return to the original grantor. In short, the greatest care should be taken when attempting to enforce restrictive agreements by threat of reversion of title.

Before leaving the matter of enforcement notice should be given to a clause frequently found which states that failure to take action against violation of a covenant shall not be considered a waiver of the right to do so thereafter. This is an attempt to escape a charge of laches. The courts, however, seem inclined to regard an omission of enforcement as acquiescence in the violation and therefore to refuse to grant relief in the future.[26] On the other hand, cases may be found where courts have handed down opposite rulings.[27]

Maintenance Charges

The purpose of maintenance charges is to secure funds for the general upkeep and to improve the appearance of the subdivision. They are an important adjunct to the developer's plan. Such funds are particularly necessary for areas which are outside the corporate

[25] Devonshire Manor, Krenn and Dato, Chicago, Ill.

[26] *Ocean City Assn. v. Chalfant*, 65 N.J. Eq. 156, 55 Atl. 801 (1903).

[27] *Bacon v. Sandberg*, 179 Mass. 396, 60 N. E. 936 (1901); also *Zipp v. Barker*, 55 N.Y. Supp. 246 (1898).

limits of a municipality and which therefore must maintain all their own improvements. The lists of items for which these funds are to be expended differ widely but the clause reproduced here will give an idea of the nature of the expenditures covered.

"Whitcomb and Keller agree to pay their proper proportion into said fund for all the unsold lots and to apply the total fund arising from said charge, as far as the same may be sufficient, toward the payment of the so-called Maintenance Expenses incurred for the following purposes:

For lighting, improving and maintaining the streets and the parks and playgrounds, if any, maintained for the general use of owners and occupants of land included in said tract, including all grass and planted areas within the boundaries of such streets, parks and playgrounds;

For caring for vacant and unimproved land, on which said Maintenance Charge is being paid, and removing the grass and weeds therefrom;

For planting and caring for trees; For expenses incident to the examination and approval of plans as herein provided, and to the enforcement of the restrictions, conditions, covenants, easements, charges and agreements herein contained;

For taxes and assessments, if any, that may be levied by any public authority upon the parks and playgrounds now or hereafter opened, laid out or established for the general use of the owners of lots included in said tract; and

For doing any and all other things that, in the opinion of Whitcomb and Keller may be of general benefit to the property owners."[28]

The amounts and methods of assessing these charges also differ greatly. With respect to amounts, no generalization can be made. Such figures as one mill, two mills, three mills per square foot are found among the restrictions examined. In each case this amount is stated as the maximum which may be assessed during any one year. The following quotation

[28] Sunnymede, Whitcomb and Keller, South Bend, Ind.

TABLE VII. RESTRICTIVE CLAUSES PROVIDING FOR MAINTENANCE CHARGES

Name of Subdivision and Subdivider and Location	Amount	By Whom Administered
Alleghany Furnace......... Baker Estates Altoona, Pa.	20c per 100 sq. ft. (minimum)	Seller at first. Later a committee of 3 owners
Ardmore.......... J. R. Robertson & Co. Chicago, Ill.		
Arlington Park............ Laudermilk Realty Co. Chicago, Ill.		
Armour Hills............ J. C. Nichols Inv. Co. Kansas City, Mo.		
Anchorage Heights........ Anchorage, Ky.	Pro-rated	
Ashburton............ G. R. Morris Org'n. Baltimore, Md.		
Andrews Sub'n............ New Britain, Conn.	Pro-rated	By seller
Avon Center Estates....... H. F. Bowse Cleveland, Ohio		
Aspinwall Hill Sub'n........ Brookline, Mass.		
Belmont Country Club..... A. T. McIntosh Co. Chicago, Ill.		
Barton Hills.............. Ann Arbor, Mich.	Pro-rated	Corporation of owners
Best Manor.............. Fred T. Wood Co. Oakland, Cal.		
Beacon Falls.............. Beacon Falls, Conn.		
Bonelli-Adams Co......... Boston, Mass.		
Bonnycastle Terrace........ Louisville, Ky.	Equal on all lots	
Brown Section............ Thorpe Bros. Minneapolis, Minn.	1 mill per sq. ft.	Owners' Assn.
Brookline Hills Sub'n....... Brookline, Mass.		
Cuyahoga View Heights..... Hoiles & Hedden Co. Cuyahoga Falls, Ohio		
Colony Hills.............. Springfield, Mass.	10c per 100 sq. ft. per yr.	
Cityco Realty Co........... Baltimore, Md.		
Cravath Sub'n............ Locust Valley, L. I.		
Cushing's Island........... Casco Bay, Me.		
Deven Heights............ Hogle & Mawdsley Carmel, Cal.		
Devonshire Manor Annex... Krenn & Dato, Inc. Chicago, Ill.		

TABLE VII. RESTRICTIVE CLAUSES PROVIDING FOR MAINTENANCE CHARGES (*Continued*)

Name of Subdivision and Subdivider and Location	Amount	By Whom Administered
Devonshire Manor......... Krenn & Dato, Inc. Chicago, Ill.		
Diana Gardens............. S. S. Berry Chicago, Ill.		
Estudillo Estates........... Fred T. Wood Co. Oakland, Cal.		
Fairview Addition.......... Chas. P. Gray Co. Chicago, Ill.		
Fairway Section............ Thorpe Brothers Minneapolis, Minn.	1 mill per sq. ft.	Owners' Assn.
Forest Hills Gardens........ Sage Foundation Homes Long Island	2 mills per sq. ft.	Seller
Fernside.................. Fred T. Wood Co. Oakland, Cal.	1 mill per sq. ft. min.	Owners' Assn.
Freeman Sub'n............ Providence, R. I.		
Gatewood Gardens......... R. C. Erskine & Co. Seattle, Wash.		
Great Neck Hills........... Great Neck, R. I.	$2 per lot to 1926	
Glen Oaks................ Guy M. Rush Los Angeles, Cal.	3 mills per sq. ft. maximum	Homes Assn.
Guilford.................. Baltimore County, Md.	20c per 100 sq. ft. maximum	
Gwin Unit................ Fred T. Wood Co. Oakland, Cal.		
Harroun Park Sub'n........ Currier Inv. Co. Detroit, Mich.	$2 per lot per yr.	
Highland Park Add'n....... Krenn & Dato, Inc. Chicago, Ill.		
Howard-Lincoln, etc., Add'n. Krenn & Dato, Inc. Chicago, Ill.		
Hunting Ridge............ Geo. R. Morris Org'n. Baltimore, Md.		
Indian Hill Estates......... Bills Realty Co. Chicago, Ill.		
Kenilworth Hghlds. Sub'n... Wittbold Realty Co. Chicago, Ill.		
A. H. Kraus Co............ Chicago, Ill.		
Lake Wauconda........... Perry Park, Colo.		Assessed on lot owners
Laudermilk Villa.......... B. H. Laudermilk Co. Chicago, Ill.		

is fairly typical of the phraseology used in these restrictions:

"All the land shown on said map entitled St. Francis Wood Extension No. 2, whether owned by Westgate Park Company or otherwise (except streets, parks, now or hereafter opened, laid out, or established, open spaces maintained for the general use of owners of property shown on said map, and land taken or sold for public improvement or uses) shall be subject to an annual charge, or assessment, of not to exceed five mills ($.005) per square foot of area. St. Francis Homes Association is hereby expressly delegated by Westgate Park Company with the sole authority to fix the rate per square foot of such charge or assessment (which shall in no event exceed five mills ($.005) and to expend for the purposes hereinafter specified the money paid in on such charges or assessments. The right to collect and enforce the collection of such charges or assessments is hereby retained by Westgate Park Company until said right is transferred by it to St. Francis Homes Association."[29]

Lack of uniformity also exists with reference to the methods of assessment. Two methods predominate: the one, already referred to, of a definite charge per unit of measurement and the other a flat charge per lot per year. Furthermore, the units of measurement vary, including frontage as a base or total number of square feet. Using either of these measurements as a base, this method of calculating the maintenance charge is superior to the flat rate. It distributes the burden more nearly in proportion to the benefits derived. A third method of figuring the maintenance charge may be mentioned. This method uses the valuation fixed by the tax assessors as the base. This procedure has particular value when the subdivision is not within the corporate limits of a municipality and is therefore subject only to state and county taxes. As a safeguard it is usually best in such

[29] St. Francis Wood, Mason-McDuffie Co., San Francisco, Cal.

cases to insert a clause in the restriction to the effect that the maintenance charge shall not exceed the tax levied in some specified municipality in the state.

The administration of these funds is another point to be considered. In a good many cases, such as the one quoted above, the subdivider reserves the power of collecting and expending the funds. On the other hand, numerous examples of the exercise of such powers by the owners' association are found. In fact, this duty is frequently one of the first responsibilities placed upon such organizations. When owners' associations have only a limited number of functions to perform, the administration of the maintenance charges is usually one of them.

From the legal point of view, these charges seem to rest on sound precedent. They are legally collectible and may be a legitimate lien upon the land. An opinion of a Missouri court illustrates the general attitude on this point.

"From what has been said it must necessarily follow that the action of the Board of Clifton Heights in levying an assessment of five dollars on part of lot thirty-eight and three dollars on part of lot thirty-seven of which defendant was at that time the owner, under and by virtue of their powers and authority contained in said deed from Kennedy and Plunkett to Fry, Tebbetts and others, was a legal and valid assessment, and the judgment rendered in pursuance thereof, declaring the same to be a first lien upon the property owned by defendant, Annex Realty Company is a legal and valid judgment and should be affirmed."[30]

The importance of considering maintenance charges has not been sufficiently emphasized either in subdivision practice or in the literature on subdivision activities. A recent tendency has been noticed in the field of city planning to lay greater emphasis on the problem of

[30] *Stevens v. Annex Realty Company*, 173 Mo. 511 (1900).

TABLE VII. RESTRICTIVE CLAUSES PROVIDING FOR MAINTENANCE CHARGES (*Continued*)

Name of Subdivision and Subdivider and Location	Amount	By Whom Administered
Lake Shore Highlands, Oakland, Cal.		
Locust Hills, Blair Home Co., Altoona, Pa.		
Licton Springs Pk., Seattle, Wash.		50c per front ft. per yr. minimum
Maple Hill, F. B. McKibbin Co., Lansing, Mich.		
Manito Park, Spokane, Wash.		
Justin Matthews Co., Little Rock, Ark.		
Milwaukee-Howard Sub'n, Krenn & Dato, Inc., Chicago, Ill.		
Mountain Lake, Lake Wales, Fla.	Pro-rated	
Morningside Heights, R. C. Erskine & Co., Seattle, Wash.		
Newton Blvd. Sub'n, Newton, Mass.		
Oak Hill Village, Arnold Hartman, Boston, Mass.		
Oyster Harbor, Inc., F. W. Norris Co., Boston, Mass.		
Pacific Southwest Bank, Los Angeles, Cal.		
Palos Verdes Estates, Los Angeles, Cal.	Set by Homes Ass'n	Homes Ass'n
Redmont Park, Jemison & Co., Birmingham, Ala.		
Roland Park, Baltimore County, Md.	25c per front ft. per year	
St. Francis Wood, Mason-McDuffie Co., San Francisco, Cal.	5 mills per sq. ft. max.	Seller until assigned to Homes Ass'n
Sackett Sub'n, Louisville, Ky.		
Scarsdale Estates, New York City		
Sudbrook, Baltimore County, Md.		
Shaker Heights, Van Sweringen Co., Cleveland, Ohio		
Sunalta, Calgary, Alberta		
S. Bloomfield Highlands, Michigan Inv. Co., Detroit, Mich.	7½c per 100 sq. ft. to 1935	
Sunrise Addition, R. C. Erskine & Co., Seattle, Wash.		

TABLE VII. RESTRICTIVE CLAUSES PROVIDING FOR MAINTENANCE CHARGES (*Continued*)

Name of Subdivision and Subdivider and Location	Amount	By Whom Administered
Sunnymede. Whitcomb & Keller South Bend, Ind.	15c per front ft. per year	Seller
Sunnyside. City Housing Corp. New York City	Payable until 1-1-1966	
Tavern Acres. No. Andover, Mass.		
Tilden Realty Corp. Utica, N. Y.		
Sunset Hill. J. C. Nichols Inv. Co. Kansas City, Mo.	Provisions in individual deeds or contracts	
Uplands. Victoria, B. C.	50c per front ft. minimum	
Uplands. Wellesley, Mass.		
Valencia Park. Bowie & Trent San Benito, Tex.		
Vanderlip Sub'n. Scarborough, N. Y.	Pro-rated	
Vinsetta Park Sub'n. Vinsetta Land Co. Detroit, Mich.	1 mill per sq. ft. for 5 yrs.	Seller
Wagner-Thoreson Co. Los Angeles, Cal.		
Woodmar. Woodmar Realty Co. Hammond, Ind.		
Westchester. William Zelosky Chicago, Ill.		
Westwood Sub'n. Van Alstine Land Co. Detroit, Mich.	$1 per lot per yr. to 1925	Seller

financing city plans. Many instances could be cited of elaborate city plans which have been drawn up during a flurry of planning enthusiasm but which are still on paper or, worse still, standing in a half-completed condition as a mockery to the planning idea.

A similar situation exists with regard to some subdivisions. Almost any city can afford at least one example of a subdivision with crumbling entrance gates or parkways grown up in weeds because inadequate provision was made for their development or upkeep. Such things are poor business from the subdivider's point of view. They represent promises unkept and cause unfavorable reactions on the part of prospective purchasers of the last lots from which the developer expects to reap his profit.

Recent awakening to the importance of the financial aspect of city planning augurs well for the future. It is to be hoped that a similar tendency will be found in the field of subdivision developments. Purchasers of subdivision property should seek assurance that the plans proposed for the development will be carried out, at least in so far as the financial means for their execution are concerned.

Miscellaneous Restrictions

Two items remain to be discussed under this heading: the organization and powers of owners' associations and the matter of reference in deeds to zoning regulations.

The formation of owners' associations to look after community affairs seems to be a comparatively new development, at least if the sample analyzed here may be considered representative. Of the older subdivisions referred to as the Olmsted group only one carried a provision for the formation of an association of lot owners and this one is a recent development, originating in 1922.[31] But among the subdivisions referred to as the newer group a number of instances of this type of organization are found.

In some instances the owners' association (or homes association, improvement association, or community association, as it is variously called) is not formed until after a certain percentage of the lots in the subdivision has been sold. The theory behind this practice is that control by a single legal entity (the subdivider) is simpler and more efficient

[31] Barton Hills, Ann Arbor, Mich.

during the early stages of development. The argument is advanced to the effect that it is difficult to get a community organization to function when there are only a few scattered lot owners. On the other side is the argument that the subdivider's interest weakens as his financial burdens become less and he is tempted to let up on restrictions in order to dispose of the balance of his lots. In other words, the interest of the home owners' association is permanent as opposed to the temporary interest of the developer.

Examining further the restrictions providing for the organization of a homes association after a certain portion of the lots is sold, it is found that the initiative for such organization originates sometimes with the subdivider and sometimes with the lot owners. Quotations from two deeds will illustrate this point:

"When eighty per cent. (80%) of the lots in said section have been sold, the Vendor, at its option, may organize an Improvement Association composed entirely of lot owners in said section and shall appoint a committee of four (4) owners in said section—one for a term of one (1) year, one for a term of two (2) years and one for a term of three (3) years, who shall be known as active members; and a fourth member who shall be known as an inactive member, who will automatically become an active member whenever a vacancy, from any cause whatsoever, shall occur among its three active members. When such fourth member becomes an active member, then the majority of the owners who are members of said Improvement Association may appoint a lot owner as the inactive member to fill the vacancy of such fourth member; but in the event of the failure of such member of the Improvement Association to make such appointment within thirty (30) days after such vacancy occurs, then the remaining three members of such committee shall have the power to appoint an owner of a lot in said section to fill such vacancy. All appointments shall be made in writing and a record kept with said Association. The majority of said committee shall have the same power as if they had been named by the Vendor herein. This committee shall have the right of approval or disapproval as in this paragraph provided, and when so organized and operative, the Vendor herein shall be relieved and released from any and all liability in connection with such duties."[32]

"Should two-thirds of the lot owners of the Maple Hill Subdivision determine upon the formation of a Community Association to administer all affairs of the owners and occupants of said subdivision, then the owner of each lot shall become a member and take out one membership for each lot and have voting power in accordance therewith."[33]

Both of these methods, however, seem inadequate, not only with respect to their origination but also with respect to their form of organization when similar provisions in the Palos Verdes agreement are examined.

It is possible here only to summarize briefly the Palos Verdes method because of its great length and detail. The Palos Verdes Homes Association[34] is an incorporated "non-stock, non-profit body under the laws of California." Its affairs are governed by a board of directors and each lot purchaser automatically becomes a member upon the receipt of his deed. The Association is charged with the enforcement of the restrictive covenants; together with the Art Jury it approves building plans as well as subdivision plans; it administers the maintenance charges; and is responsible for the general improvement and upkeep of the subdivision.

A somewhat different situation is present in the Shaker Heights development near Cleveland, Ohio. The area is an incorporated village, and, while the subdivider still retains many of his powers, the lot owners determine many of their

[32] Brown Section, Thorpe Bros., Minneapolis, Minn.

[33] Maple Hill, F. B. McKibbin, Lansing, Mich.

[34] See Protective Restrictions Palos Verdes Estates, Los Angeles County, California. Tract 7333 and Tract 8652, Montemalaga.

community affairs through the political organization.

Associations of this type seem more nearly adequate to safeguard the interests of the lot owners. Their success is dependent, however, upon the development of an active community spirit which is difficult both to develop and to maintain. Furthermore, they require considerable activity on the part of the lot owners, who do not as a rule wish to be bothered with details about their residential property. It would seem logical, therefore, that the changes to be expected in the mechanics of organization of the association would be in the direction of greater simplicity. At any rate changes are sure to take place because home owners' associations are a relatively new creation.

A final consideration is the reference in deeds to zoning ordinances which exist at the time of development or which may be inaugurated at a future date. The purpose of such reference in the deed is largely to protect the developer against possible contingencies which may arise, for interactions do take place between deed restrictions and zoning regulations, as will be pointed out later. The usual form of such reference to zoning regulations is merely a statement to the effect that the lot purchaser takes title "subject to the following covenants, conditions and restrictions, including zoning and building ordinances."

In concluding the discussion in Chapters IV and V it should be pointed out that the analysis has not been exhaustive. A number of other restrictions in addition to those treated here are contained in these deeds. The purpose has been to confine attention to those restrictive clauses which exercise the greatest control upon land development.

Furthermore, it is not possible to deduce any very satisfactory conclusions from this study as to which of these restrictions are most helpful in sales promotion or which of them are likely to arouse "sales resistance." Generalizations on such matters are extremely difficult because conditions in local markets vary so greatly. In some localities subdividers literally sell the restrictions themselves. The sales value of particular restrictions is therefore better secured from subdividers who are familiar with local real estate conditions, as influenced by the psychology of the individual buyers and by subdivision practice in that region.

CHAPTER VI

A Valuation of Deed Restrictions as a Control Device

As stated at the outset, deed restrictions are important because they define and control the relationships between the subdivider and the lot purchaser. These relationships are expressed in a transaction involving a piece of land, as a result of which both parties expect to receive certain desired returns. It is well, therefore, first to consider briefly what the subdivider and the lot purchaser are seeking from this transaction. Evaluation of restrictive agreements can then be made on the basis of whether or not they aid or hinder the securing of these ends.

For the purpose of arriving at the aims of the subdivider and the lot purchaser, two assumptions are made. It is assumed here that the subdivider is seeking, not merely to dispose of lots, but to lay the foundation for a community of homes, what has been called here a "subdivision development." For the lot purchaser it is assumed that he is buying a lot for use as a home site, and not for speculative purposes.

In the light of these assumptions three aims of the subdivider may be distinguished. He is seeking (1) the highest possible prices for his lots consistent with (2) quick turnover of the subdivision property, and (3) a complete and economical development. The last item includes substantial and attractive structures, protection against inharmonious uses both within and without the area, and economies of improvement.

To say that the subdivider is seeking the highest possible price for his lots seems to beg the question. Yet there are certain rather definite limitations on the prices he may or should ask. His main consideration is not to set a price so high that, if reselling begins, it will undermine the balance of his sales. If the subdivider seeks both high prices and quick turnover, this seems at first thought equivalent to riding two horses in opposite directions at the same time, for higher prices tend to curtail effective demand. But the subdivider may attempt to avoid this result in two different ways. After examining real estate market conditions he may figure that business is going to improve and he will thus be able to make quick sales while also securing relatively high prices. He has also another alternative. He may create a commodity which will have such a strong appeal to a specific income group that he will be able to dispose of his lots quickly at increased prices. In other words, although the increased price may cut down the *general* effective demand, the specialized character of the commodity may increase the demand of a particular income group and thus make it possible to secure high prices and quick turnover at the same time. The difficulty of striking the proper balance to secure both these objectives is obvious.

The lot purchaser would also like to profit from an increase in land values, although this may be a secondary consideration with him. Under the assumptions stated, he is primarily concerned with securing the relative permanency of his investment, and its protection against the deteriorating influence of undesirable neighbors or inharmonious uses. Finally, he is seeking amenities for his home site, in the shape of attractive surroundings.

How economically do restrictions in deeds secure these ends? The statement is often made that deed restrictions increase the value of the restricted property. But is this unqualifiedly true? It does seem to be true, if the restrictions are carefully drawn, for the early years during which the restrictions are in operation; the assurance of protection against inharmonious uses is a marketable quality, having a distinct value. Or this increased value of restricted property may arise from the scarcity of properties of this class. But whether the added value is the result of increased utility arising out of greater desirability or whether it is a scarcity phenomenon makes little difference. The subdivider is concerned with the increased value as such and is satisfied that deed restrictions contribute to that value.

The case of the lot purchaser is different. He hopes for increased value in the future, when the property shifts to a higher use. For him, then, deed restrictions may be an obstacle, particularly if they are drawn for too long a period. In order to secure the increased value desired by the lot purchaser it is necessary that the restriction be drawn in such a way as to strike the proper balance between a maximum of amenities and a minimum of injury through precluded uses in the future. Because of the great difficulties involved in establishing their proper duration, deed restrictions may work against the securing of an increased value from change of use. Furthermore, restrictive clauses tend to reduce the speculative element in subdivision property because they establish specified uses of the land for definite periods of time and thus preclude immediate turnover for another use. Finally, a restriction which has been broken may hamper sale of the property. The clause remains on record to confront the prospective purchaser even though it may long since have become a dead letter. It thus impairs the marketability of the property. In short, deed restrictions are more important to the lot purchaser from the point of view of stabilizing both the use and value of his lot than of enhancing its value. This, after all, is the important consideration when the assumption is made, as here, that he purchases for use and not for speculation.

The subdivider's second aim is rapid turnover. Restrictive covenants may both help and hinder him here. In the first place, comprehensive restrictions applied to a subdivision may tend to reduce the number of purchasers who are available for that property. The appeal is likely to be to a smaller group. However, other important factors enter into the consideration. The condition of the local market is of prime importance. If there is a dearth of subdivision property of the class which is being created under restrictions, then the limiting effect of these agreements might not be felt. In this case the restrictive clauses may promote more rapid turnover.

Paralleling this aim of the subdivider is the desire of the lot owner for protection of his investment. He seeks protection first against undesirable neighbors and here he must rely upon deed restrictions alone, for only by contractual agreements of this kind can such protection be secured. Secondly, he seeks protection against inharmonious uses and deed restrictions are only partially successful for this purpose. The potential inclusiveness of restrictive clauses can give him greater protection within the subdivision than he can secure from any other means of control. But deed restrictions control only a limited area and inharmonious uses encroaching to the very boundaries of the subdivision may cast their shadows within its borders. For securing permanency of investment, restrictions properly drawn may be said to be adequate. The lot owner is usually concerned only with a period corresponding to the span of his own life and, as stated previously, it is possible for restrictive clauses to secure protection for at least a generation. This point should, of course, be considered in relation to the problem of the duration period and its connection with the growth of the community as a whole.

Protection of investment also involves problems of enforcement. One of the weaknesses of restrictions has been the fact that their enforcement has depended upon private initiative. If individuals were lax in assuming responsibility, enforcement suffered. The weakness of the subdivider as the enforcing agent was mentioned previously as another illustration of the inadequacy of deed restrictions to protect the investment. The increasing use of legally constituted home owners' associations promises to reduce these weaknesses supposed to be inherent in restrictive clauses.

Finally, in connection with the investment aspect is the consideration of the effect of deed restrictions on borrowing. The presence of conditions subsequent in deeds is frequently an obstacle to the owner who wishes to borrow with the lot as security. Some insurance companies are especially particular on this point and often will not lend money upon property so restricted because they regard the title as too insecure. This is especially true in cases where the insurance company is in a distant city and does not know the local situation with regard to the property to be mortgaged. Restrictive covenants, on the other hand, may or may not be obstacles to borrowing. Banks and insurance companies are beginning to take precautions against lending on property which does not comply strictly with the regulations set forth in its deed, but when these covenants are carefully observed, they seem to be no hindrance to borrowing.

With respect to the third aims of both the subdivider and the lot purchaser—complete and economical development and amenities, respectively—there can be little doubt as to the effectiveness of deed restrictions in securing these ends. From the point of view of the subdivider careful observance of well-framed agreements will result in good development in the early stages which may help in the rapid disposal of the balance of the lots, wherein the profit for the developer lies. It is generally said that the returns from the sale of the last fourth of the lots constitute the profits to the subdivider. The returns from the sale of the first three-fourths are required to meet the expenses of the development process. From the point of view of the lot purchaser the adaptability of deed restrictions to fit particular situations affords opportunity for securing the maximum amenities which a given site is capable of producing.

Deed Restrictions and Zoning Compared

No discussion of deed restrictions is complete without at least some comparison of them with zoning regulations. It is not proposed to go into this question exhaustively here but only to make a few comparisons and indicate briefly some of the relationships between the two forms of control.

Such a comparison, however, introduces a new element. Up to this point deed restrictions have been evaluated only in terms of their effect upon relationships between the subdivider and the lot purchaser. To compare them with zoning it is necessary to take a public point of view, instead of the point of view of the limited group concerned in the transaction.

The differences between the two methods of control are more or less familiar and may be gone over hastily. The fact that zoning comprehends a larger area than do restrictive covenants is obvious, as are certain marked advantages accruing from systematic control as well as from this larger sphere of influence. But the very fact that zoning does deal with large areas creates serious problems. The mapping of use districts requires the utmost care on the part of zoning authorities, particularly where one district borders on another. In such cases the drafters of the zone plan should scrutinize each step lest they lay themselves open to the charge of arbitrary action. The recent decision of the United States Supreme Court in *Nectow* v. *The City of Cambridge, Massachusetts*[1] emphasized this point again. Zoning control, while recognized by the courts to be legitimate and desirable, must be applied with painstaking care lest it be attacked as an unreasonable exercise of the police power. Even though it does deal with relatively large areas, the details of its application are very important, particularly in border line cases.

A second point of comparison between zoning and restrictive covenants in deeds is their relative flexibility. Deed restrictions are said to be rigid because they endure for a specified length of time. It should be recalled in this connection that in addition to the provisions stating the duration of the restriction the conveyances usually contain two other clauses of equal importance: one providing for its extension if desired by a certain proportion of the lot owners and the other providing for annullment of the restrictions on consent of the lot owners.[2] In other words, the same instrument which states the life of the restrictive clauses provides for their modification. The courts also may supply flexibility to the operation of deed restrictions by upholding or refusing to uphold deed restrictions according to conditions prevailing in the district in question. In short, deed restrictions are not the ironclad rules they are often accused of being. Zoning regulations, on the other hand, are said to be flexible as a result of certain discretionary powers resting in the board of appeals or legislative powers residing in the city council. But this very amendibility of zoning ordinances may constitute a weakness, particularly if it is a loophole for political manipulation. Moreover, there is the difficult problem of amending a comprehensive scheme, at the same time keeping its comprehensive character.

Flexibility may, however, be used in a different sense, adaptability to individual situations. In that sense deed restrictions are unquestionably more flexible than zoning. Instead of consisting of blanket regulations applicable to all properties alike as zoning must be, restrictive clauses may be adapted to different kinds of developments. Many or few may be the restrictions included in a deed according to the type of development desired. Zoning, on the other hand, supplies uniform rules for each type of use district and because of this limitation we may expect deed restrictions to continue as important instruments supplementing and refining the zone classifications.

On the point of extensivity deed re-

[1] No. 509, U. S. Sup. Ct.; 72 L. ed.; 48 Sup. Ct. Rep. (Decided May 14, 1928).

[2] See pp. 59–62.

strictions have a distinct advantage over zoning, for they may include several types of regulations which are at present barred to zoning. Racial segregation and control of the aesthetics of private developments are the two most important items in this connection.

But more important than the differences between deed restrictions and zoning are the relationships between them, for they are frequently found in operation at the same time and on the same piece of property. The statement has been made that

"No private restrictions need ever refer to zoning, nor need any zoning ordinance ever refer to private restrictions. They are entirely separate and apart. Courts will not usually listen to the private restrictions in trying a zoning case, nor to the zoning regulations in trying a private restrictions case. They go hand in hand with each other and never conflict."[3]

But experience and recent court decisions do not support this statement. Deed restrictions may affect zoning regulations and vice versa.

The interrelation is evidenced first in the fact that both zoning ordinances and deed restrictions frequently mention the other form of control. Typical of the deed restrictions referring to zoning is the clause stating that "the above described property shall also be subject to building and zoning ordinances now in force or to be put in force."[4] Zoning ordinances, on the other hand, often state that they do not annul or abrogate any covenant or agreement[5] but some are more specific in their pronouncements, and emphasize the interrelation between zoning and deed restrictions.

[3] E. M. Bassett, Discussion, *Planning Problems*, Papers and Discussions, National Conference on City Planning, 1926, p. 71.

[4] Arthur T. McIntosh, Belmont Country Club Addition, Chicago, Ill.

[5] *Kramer v. Nelson*, 189 Wis. 560 (1926); *Welch v. Swasey*, 193 Mass. 364 at 371 (1907).

For example, the Zoning Commission Act for the District of Columbia contains the following:

"This act shall not abrogate or annul any easements, covenants or other agreements between parties: Provided, however, that as to all future building construction or use of premises where this Act or any orders or regulations adopted under the authority thereof impose a greater restriction upon the use of buildings or premises or upon height of buildings, or requires larger open spaces than are imposed or required by existing law, regulations, or permits, or by such easements, covenant, or agreements, the provision of this act and of the orders and regulations made thereunder shall control."[6]

But more important than the fact of interrelation is the question of what rules are being worked out with respect to the dominance of one form or the other. The litigated cases in which such rules will be evolved are still too few to afford any conclusive statements but certain facts and tendencies are worthy of note.

Take the case of an area which has been developed as a high-class residential district as the result of carefully drawn deed restrictions. It is not uncommon for framers of zoning ordinances to respect this development in their plans whenever possible. In one case the zoning authorities went even further. On the theory that property owners who have long complied with restrictions as to residential use deserve protection the drafters of the zone plan extended the residential area to include land not originally restricted to that use. A permit to build an apartment on this additional residential land was then refused on the ground that it would constitute a nuisance to those who had built in accordance with the restrictions.[7] This is a case of a zoning ordinance

[6] Quoted in *Castleman v. Avignone*, 56 D. C. App. 253, at 259, (1926).

[7] *Minkus v. Pond*, 326 Ill. 467, 158 N. E. 121 (1927).

supporting and extending the plan inaugurated under deed restrictions.

Much more difficult are the problems where the standards of the two control devices are different. When the zoning ordinance establishes higher standards than the restrictive covenants, no particular problem is involved, for in that case the ordinance is meeting no different situation than it does in application to unrestricted properties.[8]

But a very different situation exists when the deed restrictions are more severe than zoning regulations. Can a zoning ordinance legalize a lower use of the property than that permitted by the restrictive agreement? Does the classification of property for business use by a zoning ordinance require the owners thereof so to use it? The consensus of opinion in the few recent cases available on the question is negative. A leading case is that of *Ludgate* v. *Somerville*[9]. Both plaintiff and defendant owned lots in a subdivision restricted to residential use. Subsequently a zoning ordinance was enacted which permitted business of certain kinds in this district. The defendant wanted to erect a filling station on his property and the plaintiff sought an injunction on the ground that it violated the restriction. Three points in the opinion reveal the attitude of the court. The character of the district was one consideration. The injunction was granted mainly on the ground that the character of the district had not so changed as to make the operation of the restrictive covenant inequitable. A New York court in a case[10] decided a year previously had refused an injunction against the erection of a business building on a site restricted to residential use. Various grounds were cited, including the fact that the restriction had but two more years to run and that the plaintiff's gain would not be at all commensurate with the defendant's loss because the character of the district had so changed that enforcement of the restriction would not restore the original condition of the neighborhood. This matter of the "character of the district" is one of the focal points about which disputes between zoning ordinances and deed restrictions will probably revolve. The courts examine carefully the present circumstances in the area in question and on this basis decide whether a change in use is desirable. In general it may be said that the courts are not likely to encourage more rapid change from one use to another than would take place in the normal course of events.

A second consideration in the *Ludgate* v. *Somerville* opinion involved the relation of police power regulations to existing lawful agreements. The court stated that "the police power is not to be exercised to thwart or nullify lawful agreements which in no way operate to the detriment of the public welfare."[11] A similar statement is found in an Illinois case.

> "Notwithstanding said ordinance the owners of said lots have the constitutional right to make use of them in accordance with such restrictions, so long as they do not endanger or threaten the safety, health and comfort or general welfare of the public."[12]

The third point of significance in the Oregon opinion is the statement to the effect that restrictive agreements give the property owner rights which cannot be divested by such legislation as a zoning ordinance. Here again an interesting parallel is found, this time in a Massachusetts opinion which states that

[8] See n. 7.

[9] 121 Ore. 643, 256 Pac. 1043 (1927).

[10] *Forstmann v. Joray Holding Co.*, 244 N. Y. 22 (1926).

[11] *Supra* n. 9 at 1045.

[12] *Gordon v. Caldwell*, 235 Ill. App. 170 (1924).

the zoning law cannot constitutionally relieve land within the district covered by it from lawful restrictions affecting its use . . .[13] Although the evidence is scanty, the conclusion may be reached from the cases cited that the courts consider restrictive covenants as creating property rights which are enforceable so long as they do not contravene the public welfare and are not inequitable in their operation.

The legal problems involved in the relationship between zoning and deed restrictions are only just coming to the fore.[14] Zoning is still in the experimental stage. Its relation to deed restrictions and other older forms of control has still to be worked out. The significance of the relatively new device, the subdivision control ordinance, is not yet clear. It may be that such ordinances will afford the means of adjustment between the various devices for regulating the development of urban areas.

The fact remains, however, that deed restrictions seem likely to continue for some time to be an important force in controlling the development of urban land. They constitute a control device which is available to all and which is adaptable to a variety of situations. But more important is the established legal status of deed restrictions. The attitude of the courts is fairly clearly defined in all jurisdictions, and subdividers and purchasers are familiar with this method of control and feel confident of its permanency and soundness.

[13] *Vorenberg v. Bunnell*, 257 Mass. 399, 153 N. E. 884, at 887 (1926).

[14] See M. T. Van Hecke, "Zoning Ordinances and Restrictions in Deeds", 37 *Yale Law Journal* 407-425 (February, 1928). This article, which is written from the zoning point of view, is an able discussion of the uses to which each of these control devices may be put, the administrative methods of each and the effect of one upon the other.

TABLE OF DEEDS ANALYZED

Alleghany Furnace, Baker Estates, Altoona, Pa.
Ardmore, J. R. Robertson & Co., Chicago, Ill.
Arlington Park, Bert H. Laudermilk Realty Ass'n, Chicago, Ill.
Armour Hills, J. C. Nichols Inv. Co., Kansas City, Mo.
Anchorage Heights, Anchorage, Ky.
Ashburton, G. R. Morris Org'n., Baltimore, Md.
Andrews Subdivision, New Britain, Conn.
Avon Center Estates, H. F. Bowse, Cleveland, Ohio.
Aspinwall Hill Subdivision, Brookline, Mass.
Barton Hills, Ann Arbor, Mich.
Best Manor, Fred T. Wood Co., Oakland, Cal.
Beacon Falls, Beacon Falls, Conn.
Belmont Country Club, A. T. McIntosh Co., Chicago, Ill.
Bonelli-Adams Co., Boston, Mass.
Bonnycastle Terrace, Louisville, Ky.
Brown Section, Thorpe Bros., Minneapolis, Minn.
Brookline Hills Subdivision, Brookline,
Cityco Mass. Realty Co., Baltimore, Md.
Cuyahoga View Heights, Hoiles & Hedden Co., Cuyahoga Falls, Ohio.
Colony Hills, Springfield, Mass.
Cravath Subdivision, Locust Valley, L. I.
Cushings Island, Casco Bay, Me.
Deven Heights, Hogle and Mawdsley, Carmel, Cal.
Devonshire Manor Annex, Krenn & Dato, Inc., Chicago, Ill.
Devonshire Manor, Krenn & Dato, Inc., Chicago, Ill.
Diana Gardens, S. S. Berry, Chicago, Ill.
Estudillo Estates, Fred T. Wood Co., Oakland, Cal.
Fairview Addition, Chas. P. Gray Co., Chicago, Ill.
Fairway Section, Thorpe Bros., Minneapolis, Minn.
Forest Hills Gardens, Sage Foundation Homes, L. I.
Fernside, Fred T. Wood Co., Oakland, Cal.
Freeman Subdivision, Providence, R. I.
Gatewood Gardens, R. C. Erskine & Co., Seattle, Wash.
Great Neck Hills, Great Neck, L. I.
Glen Oaks, Guy M. Rush, Los Angeles, Cal.
Guilford, Baltimore County, Md.
Gwin Unit, Fred T. Wood Co., Oakland, Cal.
Harroun Park Subdivision, Currier Investment Co., Detroit, Mich.
Highland Park Addition, Krenn & Dato, Inc., Chicago, Ill.
Howard-Lincoln Subdivision, Krenn & Dato, Inc., Chicago, Ill.
Hunting Ridge, Geo. R. Morris Org'n., Baltimore, Md.
Indian Hill Estates, Bills Realty Co., Chicago, Ill.
Kenilworth Highlands Subdivision, Wittbold Realty Co., Chicago, Ill.
A. H. Kraus Co., Chicago, Ill.
Lake Wauconda, Perry Park, Colo.
Laudermilk Villa, Bert H. Laudermilk Realty Ass'n, Chicago, Ill.
Lake Shore Highlands, Oakland, Cal.
Locust Hills, Blair Home Co., Altoona, Pa.
Licton Springs Park, Seattle, Wash.
Maple Hill, F. B. McKibbin Co., Lansing, Mich.
Manito Park, Spokane, Wash.
Justin Matthews Co., Little Rock, Ark.
Milwaukee-Howard-Harlem Subdivision, Krenn & Dato, Inc., Chicago, Ill.
Mountain Lake, Lake Wales, Florida
Morningside Heights, R. C. Erskine & Co., Seattle, Wash.
Newton Blvd. Subdivision, Newton, Mass.
Oak Hill Village, Arnold Hartman, Boston, Mass.
Oyster Harbor, Inc., F. W. Norris Co., Boston, Mass.
Pacific Southwest Bank, Los Angeles, Cal.
Palos Verdes Estates, Los Angeles, Cal.
Redmont Park, Jemison & Co., Birmingham, Ala.
Roland Park, Baltimore County, Md.
St. Francis Wood, Mason-McDuffie Co., San Francisco, Cal.
Sackett Subdivision, Louisville, Ky.
Scarsdale Estates, New York City
Sudbrook, Baltimore County, Md.
Shaker Heights, Van Sweringen Co., Cleveland, Ohio
Sunalta, Calgary, Alberta
Sunrise Addition, R. C. Erskine & Co., Seattle, Wash.
Sunnymede, Whitcomb & Keller, South Bend, Ind.
Sunnyside, City Housing Corp., New York City
Tavern Acres, N. Andover, Mass.

Tilden Realty Corp., Utica, N. Y.
S. Bloomfield Highlands, Michigan Inv. Co., Detroit, Mich.
Sunset Hill, J. C. Nichols Inv. Co., Kansas City, Mo.
Uplands, Victoria, B. C.
Uplands, Wellesley, Mass.
Valencia Park, Bowie & Trent, San Benito, Tex.
Vanderlip Subdivision, Scarborough, N. Y.
Vinsetta Park Subdivision, Vinsetta Land Co., Detroit, Mich.
Wagner-Thoreson Co., Los Angeles, Cal.
Woodmar, Woodmar Realty Co., Hammond, Ind.
Westchester, William Zelosky, Chicago, Ill.
Westwood Subdivision, Van Alstine Land Co., Detroit, Mich.

TABLE OF CASES CITED

Allen v. *City of Detroit*, 167 Mich. 464 (1911)
Anderson v. *Stewart*, 285 Ill. 605 (1918)
Bacon v. *Sandberg*, 179 Mass. 396, 60 N. E. 93 (1901)
Berryman v. *Hotel Savoy Co.*, 160 Cal. 559 (1911)
Buchanan v. *Warley*, 245 U. S. 60 (1917)
Castleman v. *Avignone*, 56 App. D. C. 253 (1926)
Columbia College v. *Thatcher*, 87 N. Y. 311 (1882)
Cooperative Vineyards Co. v. *Ft. Stockton Irrigated Lands Co.*, 158 S. W. 1191 (Tex. Civ. App. 1913)
Corrigan v. *Buckley*, 271 U. S. 323, 70 L. ed. 969 (1925)
Cowell v. *Colorado Springs Co.*, 100 U. S. 55 (1879)
Curtis v. *Rubin*, 244 Ill. 88 (1910)
Druecker v. *McLaughlin*, 235 Ill. 367, 85 N. E. 647 (1908)
Easterbrook v. *Hebrew L. Orphan Soc.*, 85 Conn. 289 (1912)
Eckhart v. *Irons*, 128 Ill. 568 (1889)
Erichsen v. *Tapert*, 172 Mich. 457 (1912)
Ewersten v. *Gerstenberg*, 186 Ill. 344 (1900)
Forstmann v. *Joray Holding Co.*, 244 N. Y. 22 (1926)
Frye v. *Partridge*, 82 Ill. 267 (1876)
Godley v. *Weisman*, 113 Minn. 1 (1916)
Gordon v. *Caldwell*, 235 Ill. App. 170 (1924)
Harmon v. *Burow*, 263 Pa. 188 (1919)
Henderson v. *Champion*, 83 N. J. Eq. 554, 91 Atl. 332 (1914)
Highland Realty Co. v. *Groves*, 130 Ky. 374, 113 S. W. 420 (1908)
Hutchinson v. *Ulrich*, 145 Ill. 336 (1893)
Jackson v. *Stevenson*, 156 Mass. 496 (1892)
Janss Investment Co. v. *Walden*, 196 Cal. 753, 239 Pac. 34 (1925)
Johnson v. *Hess*, 126 Ind. 298 (1890)
Johnson v. *Jones*, 244 Pa. St. 386 (1914)
Jones v. *Northwest Real Estate Co.*, 149 Md. 271, 131 Atl. 446 (1925)
Jones v. *Port Huron Engine Co.*, 171 Ill. 502 (1898)
Judd v. *Robinson*, 41 Colo. 222 (1907)
Killien v. *Goodman*, 229 Mich. 393 (1924)
Kneip v. *Schroeder*, 255 Ill. 621 (1912)
Koch v. *Streuter*, 232 Ill. 594 (1908)
Koehler v. *Rowland*, 275 Mo. 573, (1918)
Kramer v. *Nelson*, 189 Wis. 560 (1926)
Landsberg v. *Rosenwasser*, 124 N. Y. App. Div. 559 (1928)
Leonard v. *Hotel Majestic Co.*, 17 N. Y. Misc. 229, 40 N. Y. Supp. 1044 (1896)
Library Neighborhood Assn. v. *Goosen*, 229 Mich. 89 (1924)
Los Angeles Investment Co. v. *Gary*, 181 Cal. 680, 186 Pac. 596 (1920)
Ludgate v. *Somerville*, 121 Ore. 643, 256 Pac. 1043 (1927)
McCusker v. *Goode*, 185 Mass. 607 (1904)
McNeil v. *Gary*, 40 App. D. C. 397 (1913)
McNichol v. *Townsend*, 73 N. J. Eq. 276 (1907)
Melson v. *Ormsby*, 169 Ia. 522 (1915)
Minard v. *Delaware, Lackawanna & Western Railroad Co.*, 139 Fed. 60 (1905)
Minkus v. *Pond*, 326 Ill. 467, 158 N. E. 121 (1927)
Mitchell v. *Leavitt*, 30 Conn. 587 (1862)
Moore v. *Curry*, 176 Mich. 456; 142 N. W. 839 (1913)
Nectow v. *City of Cambridge, Mass.*, No. 509 U. S. Sup. Ct., 72 L. ed., 48 Sup. Ct. Rep. (Decided May 14, 1928)
Ocean City Assn. v. *Chalfant*, 65 N. J. Eq. 156, 55 Atl. 801 (1903)
Page v. *Murray*, 46 N. J. Eq. 325 (1890)
Parmalee v. *Morris*, 218 Mich. 624 (1922)
Peabody Heights Co. v. *Willson*, 82 Md. 186 (1895)
Porter v. *Barrett*, 233 Mich. 373 (1925)
Post v. *Weil*, 115 N. Y. 361 (1889)
Randall v. *Atlanta Adv. Serv.*, 159 Ga. 217 (1924)
River Bank Imp. Co. v. *Bancroft*, 209 Mass. 217, 95 N. E. 216 (1911)
Sanford v. *Keer*, 80 N. J. Eq. 240, 83 Atl. 225 (1912)
Schoonmaker v. *Heckshe*r, 171 N. Y. App Div. 148, 157 N. Y. Supp. 75 (1916)
Sharp v. *Ropes*, 110 Mass. 381 (1872)
Simpson v. *Mikkelsen*, 196 Ill. 575 (1902)
Skinner v. *Shepard*, 130 Mass. 180 (1881)
Stevens v. *Annex Realty Co.*, 173 Mo. 511 (1900)
Summers v. *Beeler*, 90 Md. 475 (1899)
Van Sant v. *Rose*, 260 Ill. 401 (1913)
Vorenberg v. *Bunnell*, 257 Mass. 399, 153 N. E. 884 (1926)
Welch v. *Swasey*, 193 Mass. 364 (1907)
Wiegman v. *Kusel*, 270 Ill. 520 (1915)
Wood v. *Stehrer*, 119 Md. 143, 86 Atl. 128 (1912)
Wright v. *Pfrimmer*, 99 Neb. 447 (1916)
Zinn v. *Sidler*, 268 Mo. 680 (1916)
Zipp v. *Barker*, 55 N. Y. Supp. 246 (1898)

INDEX

Spotted something that isn't quite right?

Let us know and we'll fix it for future reprints.
And as a thank you for your diligence, we'll
send you a free Sothis book of your choice.

publisher@sothis.press

This page intentionally left blank

Except of course for that line above. And this one.
And whilst we have your attention, perhaps you'd
like to follow us on Instagram @sothis.press. Go on.

Made in United States
Orlando, FL
04 November 2026

90201168R00055